THE TURBULENT TEENS

Understanding, Helping, Surviving

DR. JAMES E. GARDNER

Sorrento Press, Inc.

Los Angeles

Published by Sorrento Press, Inc.

Library of Congress Cataloging in Publication Data

Gardner, James E.
  The turbulent teens, understanding, helping, surviving.

  1. Parenting.   2. Youth.   3. Parent and child.
I.Title.
HQ775.8.G37   649'.125   81-22442
ISBN 0-913091-01-4   AACR2

First Paperback Edition
1 2 3 4 5 6 7 8 9 85 84 83
Printed and bound in the United States of America

For Rosalind, my wife . . .

Contents

Contents

Acknowledgments

T he teenagers I have known over the years were the primary resource for this book. The needs of my own adolescents, and those with whom I have worked professionally, caused me to think carefully about the adolescent process. The teenagers taught me so much in so many ways. I can only hope that I have given something of value to them and their parents in return.

My wife, Rosalind, to whom this book is dedicated, was of inestimable assistance in a great many ways. But, most of all, she supported me emotionally over the four-year duration of this project. Roz also offered valuable insights and suggestions for the manuscript. And, as the real measure of her devotion, she typed and retyped this book again and again.

Jenny Gumpertz took these typed and retyped pages and cut, pasted, suggested, and rewrote in fine editorial fashion. I am indebted to Jenny for clarifying the substance and the style of the book. Lucky Roberts contributed his invaluable knowledge of the publishing business and his unfailing courtesy and good nature throughout.

CHAPTER 1

The Crisis Years

This book is about teenagers. It is about understanding, helping, and coping with teenagers through a difficult time of life. It is a book for parents of teenagers or others working with adolescents.

The teen years are difficult. Teenagers are hard on themselves, and they're hard on parents. They're hard on teachers and other adults whose business it is to train, coach, guide, and channel them. Teenagers tend to be a high-energy, unstable, fast-changing, self-centered, nonlogical, and generally bananas group of people.

Don't get me wrong. I like teenagers. I think they are fun to watch and often fun to be with. It is nice to observe the buddings of first love. There is *something* there when you help your son with his tie before his first big dance, or when you keep your cool more or less and help your daughter fill out one more insurance form for one more dented fender.

And yet our teenagers can bring out the worst in us. They are often hard to handle in reasonable and constructive ways. At times we can't figure out the *right* way to handle the irritating, annoying, and crazy situations they can create or stumble into. To be reasonably effective and helpful as parents we need information.

What is adolescence all about? What do you do about drugs? Is marijuana harmful? How do you punish a teenager? How do you talk sense into their heads? How do teenagers perceive themselves? Each other? The world? Why are they so often angry and surly? Why are they so moody? How can you help your teenagers grow up to be mature, happy, "together" people?

We want to help our children. But most of us do not understand our adolescent children very well. We try to help. But we often end up offering the wrong kind of help at the wrong time. The love is there, the intent is good, but things just seem to go wrong. As parents we often feel puzzled and frustrated by our teenagers, just as they do by us. Sometimes our adolescents become surly and rebellious, feeling that their parents are hopelessly old-fashioned and square.

At times, they're right about that. It's easy for some of us in the older generation to be out of step with the TV-saturated, drug-oriented, supersexualized society in which our children are growing up. They have to grapple with options, decisions, and pressures that most of us never had to face and don't understand. Today's teenagers are hard put to find structure and guidelines for growing up and getting on with life. We would help them if we could, but the gap between the generations is often too wide. We often feel exasperated rather than rewarded as our *sensible* reasoning falls on very deaf ears. Sometimes we feel like telling the young person to take a flying jump into the nearest river. More than one parent has considered the possibility of simple homicide when faced with the perplexities and general nonsense of his adolescent children.

If beating up on the kids would help, that might be a course of action to be considered. Such a tactic, however, is usually quite counterproductive, as are most forms of punishment. A more useful path for you, or any other adult concerned with teenagers, is that of simply learning more about what people of this age are going through and learning about how to be of some assistance to them on their way toward becoming "grown-ups."

One of the basic ideas of this book is that the more you know about the process of adolescent development the more helpful you can be. Some parents think that they may have "blown it" in the child's early years and there can be no making up for it later. I don't think this is so. I believe that parents can be very important to their children all the way into adulthood, and perhaps especially so in the teen years.

Throughout this book I try to provide a general picture of the adolescent phase. I also offer specific how-to-do-it suggestions and anecdotes. But no book can cover every possible situation in an area as complex as adolescent behavior. So you must examine the information and incidents and see how they apply to your own teenagers and to the situation in your own family.

One thing that will help you along the perplexing road toward your teenager's maturity is knowledge about such concepts as identity crisis, illogical thinking, and dependency vs. independence. It will help if you know something about what work, responsibility, and "the frightening future" mean to a young person.

Another basic idea in this book is that the more teenagers know about what is happening the less anxious they will be about what is going on within themselves. So even though this book is intended for you, as a parent, you might offer it to your teenager to read too. If you are on relatively good terms with your youngster, you could discuss the turmoil that goes on during adolescence, and why it does.

Adolescence can be such a confusing time. The teenager's body is changing in bewildering, though wonderful, ways. Irrational feelings and swings of mood seem to come out of nowhere. Confronting responsibilities and events may seem terrifying and may be understood only dimly.

If you think of adolescence as a tapestry of complex but not yet completed patterns, with even the adolescent not knowing where the threads are headed, then you arrive at a much better understanding of the confusions and anxieties that are a part of this period of life.

I am saying that the teen years are terribly important. They represent a hard, jarring shift from childhood to adulthood. They should be considered as *crisis years.*

If you are like most parents, you weren't really prepared for your child's adolescence. You may not have thought about what sort of person your child would become or what experiences young people face as they move into puberty and their teens.

In the beginning, you probably thought of your offspring mostly as a baby and then as a young child. Perhaps you also had some vague thoughts about early school years. Maybe you even had some hazy dreams of your child as a young adult, getting married, having babies, and becoming successful in some line of work.

To plan ahead more than five or six years is difficult for businesses, governments, and individuals alike. It is no surprise, then, that you may not have planned ten, twelve, or fifteen years ahead toward your child's teens and "the adolescent experience."

I was the same way. When I was a young man, one of my very important goals was to marry and have children. These events transpired (in that order), and I began to behave in a manner now fashionably known as "parenting."

Upon reflection now, in the middle of my life, I realize that my concept of "having children" and "parenting" was essentially limited to considerations and fantasies about the early years of my children, not of their later lives and older selves.

Occasionally, of course, my thoughts flashed forward to what it would be like to play sports with my sons, or to have some sort of special "Daddy's girl" relationship with my daughter. However, during those early years, I never thought seriously about what *kinds* of people they might eventually become as older children and teenagers. But now my children are in, or have gone through, adolescence. Also, I have worked professionally with thousands of adolescents. Although I do not know everything about teenagers (no one can), I do know some things. And I feel that what I have learned is important for you and all parents to know.

I would like to make it very clear that I do not pretend, even in my wildest fantasies of myself as a sage, that I *fully* grasp the nature of adolescence. Like the blind man attempting to understand the essence of the elephant, I have my own little patch of familiarity and knowledge, but of which end I cannot say. And while not all the ideas in this book apply to all adolescents, I trust that most of the points apply to most adolescents to some extent.

My daughter, in her first years of college and entering the late-adolescent or young-adulthood stage, to make sure her psychologist father worked under no pretensions or delusions, sent me the following poem:

There are so many things you
        don't know about me
And that I don't know
        about you

Don't ever assume you know
        what you don't
So many things have passed
        before my eyes, so many

Things I've done that I just
        can't tell you about in
One sitting or in so many words

And I'm sure you have the
        same type of things but
Half the part of a growing friendship
        relies on what one doesn't know
About the other and what one will find out
        and one will never know . . .

Following my daughter's advice, I have tried not to assume that I know what I do not know. But it is appropriate that I tell you why I may be able to contribute something to your understanding of your teenager and at the same time explain what this book is, and is not, about.

As a clinical psychologist practicing in Los Angeles and specializing with children and adolescents, I spend some 40 hours per week in my office working with young people, counseling with parents, or consulting with schools. Additionally, at least another 20 or so hours per week are spent in reading, writing, or lecturing about children and adolescents. This has been my professional life for some twenty years.

My basic knowledge about adolescent development comes primarily from two areas. The first area involves my consulting work with disturbed and nondisturbed adolescents and their families. This practical, everyday working experience has been mixed and meshed with the thoughts of others who work with this age group, and of researchers working in this field. Out of all this has come a blend of ideas about why teenagers act as they do and are as they are. These ideas, when linked together, form the beginnings of a framework in which the process of adolescent development may be better understood.

The second source of my approach to understanding the adolescent process comes from my own personal, in-depth, firsthand experience involving close encounters of all kinds with my own five children. Within my own family, virtually whatever could have happened, has happened! In the words of Steve Martin, my own are a "wild and crazy group." As Dr. Jean Piaget, the renowned Swiss psychologist, did with his children, I have observed, interacted with, thought about, and learned much from my own.

This book is part "how-to" manual and part "guidebook" through the troubled territory of adolescence. And you *do* have to learn the territory. I realize that asking people to understand the *nature* of something may be the kiss of death. This is because all of us like the quick fix, the easy solution, the direct and simple answer. I could tell you that I have easy, direct, and simple answers. This would, however, be untrue. People are very complicated. They have moods, varying backgrounds, different values, and their own ideas about the world. But if people in general are complicated, those people called teenagers are *really* complicated.

However, just because something is complicated does not mean that it cannot be, with some thought, understood.

I bought a small sailing boat some years ago. I had never owned a boat before and did not know how to sail. I took courses and read books about sailing, and others with more experience taught me how to sail. What was at first an uptight, migraine-headache-producing experience became an activity of great joy. I could sail a boat.

Granted, sailing a boat is simple when compared with guiding a teenager through the shifting currents and dark waters of today. The old landmarks are no longer there to guide us. The young people often reject religion. They put down traditional values. They are peer-oriented rather than parent-oriented. Whether this is good or bad does not really matter. As the teenagers say, "It's where it's at."

The point here is that adolescence is a very strange and very complicated time. I feel there is no more complex phase of life. So many things are going on inside young people that it boggles the mind. And it is all happening in a very short period of time. In just a few years they go from being children to being adults, from a state of almost utter dependency to being independent. No wonder there is confusion. No wonder there are problems. And no wonder that you become very frustrated with your teen-age children. Such frustration is natural. Don't feel guilty about it. We all feel the same way toward these strangers who are also our flesh and blood.

Jonathan Swift, author of *Gulliver's Travels*, once proposed satirically (with recipes) that the children of the poor in Ireland be sold to be used for food. Some people have suggested equally dire fates for teenagers, Irish or not.

A friend of mine, upon being told that I was writing a book about teenagers, stated that this would be my first attempt at a horror story. Another said that if the book was trying to help anyone with their teenagers it was a fairy tale, since such help was impossible. And at a dinner party, a noted psychologist advised me that the best way to handle adolescents would be to lock them all in a warehouse at age 12 and release them at age 20.

These facetious comments express some of the underlying ambivalence in the feelings many adults have toward adolescents. Many of the examples and comments in the book tend to deal with problems a teenager may be having with you and the other adults in his world. Other examples deal with the inner difficulties the young person must work through before moving toward a higher level of maturity.

A comment about some of the language in this book seems important here. I debated at length whether or not to censor the rougher language when I quoted some of the teenagers. Although some ears may be offended by salty language, to whitewash it was to take away from the tone and feel of the way teenagers often express themselves. So, with apologies for some of the language, I must point out that I am quoting the kids. Like it or not, that's the way they often talk.

All names and circumstances were, of course, changed in order that no individuals can be identified. For the most part, the clinical material presented represents a composite picture having to do with the problem areas experienced by many adolescents with whom I have worked over the years. My own teenagers, their friends, and many of the young people with whom I work in a counseling relationship have read and commented on the book as it progressed. Invariably, they all saw themselves in the book at one point or another, whether I had actually included them or not. I felt that this was a good sign, for it suggested that I was touching on certain universal aspects of adolescent experience in our society.

It is also important to note that I could have written a great deal about the *nonproblem* behavior of teenagers. The teen years can be a time of high idealism, beautiful friendships, and deep and meaningful relationships with others of all ages. Although I do touch on some of these areas, most of this book deals with the great psychological struggles involved in growing up during that transitional, high-stress time of life known as *adolescence.*

CHAPTER 2

Three Families: Conversations in the Consultation Room

My 14-year-old girl has no interests other than boys, the telephone, and music. She has no interest in school at all and does nothing constructive. She's often extremely argumentative and she causes a lot of tension at home. She's mean to her sister and makes her sister be her "flunky." She is constantly complaining about herself—it's either her skin breaking out, or her hair is too curly, or she's too fat, too tall, too pale, has ugly hands, a double chin, hates her clothes, hates the color of her room, hates our cars, hates the way I look and dress. Mostly, she blames her father and me for all of her problems. She's *very* trying to be with. I think I exercise *great* patience. I'm sympathetic and give her lots of time and attention. But what I'd really like to do is to tell her to SHUT-UP!

Note to me from the mother of a tall, attractive girl

We're just very confused about how to handle our son. He seems dissatisfied with school and with just about everything. He only seems to like partying. We think he's smoking marijuana and maybe using other drugs. We are so worried we are sick. His mother and I would do anything to make the boy happy—or at least feel satisfied with himself. But we don't know what to do.

Father of a teen-age boy

On this morning there are no conversations in my consultation room. It is a writing morning for me. And it is on mornings such as this, over a period of years, that this

book has emerged. Although it is quiet here today, there have been many thousands of conversations in this room. Members of many families have talked to me here and, sometimes, have also learned how to talk to each other. Since so much of my knowledge of the adolescent process has come out of my consultation work with teenagers and their families, it seems appropriate to give you a flavor of what goes on in many of those families, perhaps families very similar to yours.

During the past week I have met with each of the three families discussed in this chapter. The families are not acquainted with one another. None were referred to me by a physician or a school for having an emotionally disturbed adolescent. Yet they share the common bond of concern over a teenager. Each family had called and requested an appointment to talk about their youngster.

As you read about these teenagers and their parents, you may see traces of stresses and strains that exist within your own family, for these are not people in strange or unusual situations. They are just ordinary people who are having some problems. The parents don't understand their kids and vice versa. Communication has broken down or become increasingly negative. All members of the family are feeling frustrated and uptight with one another. They are, in other words, people just like you and me.

THE ANDERSONS

Joan and Ron Anderson asked if I would talk with them and their 16-year-old son Steve. Friction between father and son had been increasing in the past year or so. The tensions in the family were now beginning to affect Joan and Ron's relationship.

In essence, Steve wanted more freedom. He wanted more use of the family car, a later curfew, and less nagging about studying and phone calls and the like. Ron, for his part, wanted more responsibility from Steve in the matter of doing chores, getting in at a decent hour, and informing others of

his whereabouts at various times of the day or night. Joan was caught in the middle between husband and son. She felt that both Ron and Steve had valid complaints, but she felt helpless to assist in mending the deepening rift between them.

In our consultation session, after the basic issues had been stated, I suggested that Joan and I just sit quietly for a while and let Ron and Steve talk to each other. Almost at once we could see the father and son did not know how to communicate with each other. Most of their past negotiations had either been through Joan or with Joan as a buffer. Ron and Steve's talk at this point consisted of simply repeating demands, charges, and countercharges. It was apparent that neither could hear—really hear—what the other was saying. This block in communication prevented understanding, which raised their frustration levels very quickly.

Steve became angry, rude, and tearful, with flushed face and clenched fists. Ron countered Steve's petulant demands with sarcasm. Since Ron had the power to withhold the family car and other goodies, the boy would just have to knuckle under to his wishes. But in power struggles between family members, usually everyone loses. Ron might be winning the argument, but he was going to lose the boy.

Ron finally told Steve to "grow up." This seemed to touch something deep in the young man. He told his father that he did not want to grow up, that he would like to be 16 forever, and that he did not feel that he could succeed at a job. Ron replied that Steve wanted to "play without having to pay." Steve argued that he just wanted to have some fun, that he would have to work all his life so why start so soon, and, again, that he did not want to become part of the adult world with its adult responsibilities.

Steve, beginning by this point to communicate his underlying feelings more openly, went on to say that he not only did not know what he was going to do for a career, he did not know what major he should be in. And, further, he was not even sure of who he was. He felt that both of his parents were undermining him and not backing him up in any area of his

life. He expressed much resentment toward them for their lack of support.

Ron and Joan tried to defend themselves, pointing out all the ways in which they felt they had been supportive to their son. They were hurt by Steve's words and worried about his apparent low self-confidence. And they felt that they had been good parents.

Things aren't usually resolved in one conversation, no matter how promising that conversation might be. So this family will be coming to talk with me some more. Ron and Joan need to learn a good deal more about why Steve feels so resentful toward them and how to handle these feelings. All members of this family need to learn more about what is happening between parent and young person during this complicated phase of development known as adolescence. Even many normal aspects of teen-age behavior seem strange and hard to understand to many adults. In time, there is a good chance that better communication will develop between Steve and his father. Ron and Joan will eventually see that even "good" parents get a lot of blame and a lot of nonsense from their teenagers. It may not be fair, but it is simply the way things are.

THE GOLDS

Susan, a 15-year-old girl with a lovely face and figure, came to my office with her parents. The parents were upset because of reports by another girl's mother that Susan had engaged in sexual and drug experimentation at a party some weeks before. Donald, the father, found the thought of such behavior very painful. His response had been to withdraw from his daughter in hurt and anger. He had not spoken to her in weeks. Jackie, the mother, was as upset about Susan as her husband, but her reaction had been to attack. Ever since Susan's apparent misconduct surfaced, Jackie had bitterly harangued her. The mother and daughter argued, screamed, and wept for the better part of the past several days.

Initially, in our conference, the parents pressed their ac-

cusations on Susan, the father calling her a "slut" and the mother wanting me to prescribe an appropriate punishment. They went on to elaborate the reasons for their anger. Susan had always been their "good girl," an excellent student, popular, and a good athlete. She maintained an A-average, though lately her grades had become somewhat erratic. It appeared that the parents had been gradually led to expect near perfection from their daugther. They were deeply disappointed and angered because she was no longer living up to these expectations.

The parents were puzzled and frightened as well. They confessed to being at a loss about what to do. Nothing in either of their backgrounds equipped them to handle this situation. They had met in high school, gone steady, and married early. Neither had ever dated another person and neither had used drugs of any kind. To them, Susan's behavior was nothing short of shameful and sinful.

But all this didn't keep us from being able to discuss the positive aspects of Susan's character, the closeness of the family, and how difficult it is for families to maintain close and supportive ties in the modern world. Gradually, Donald and Jackie came to a position from which they could comfortably state that they wanted to understand Susan and help her. They said also that they wanted to be a part of her life and not alienate her from them.

Susan, on her part, said that she needed and wanted her parents' love and support. But, she said, they were not being understanding about the sex and drugs issue. She pointed out that the sex matter had involved some petting with a boy at the party. As for the drugs, that had consisted of smoking marijuana at the same party. She did not defend her behavior as right. Instead, she asked why her parents considered it so wrong. She accurately pointed out that many other kids her age were much more involved with both sex and drugs, that she tried to be a good daughter, but that she also had to live her own life and decide some things for herself, including making her own mistakes.

The general conversation seemed to give the parents and daughter an awareness that the girl was moving forward through adolescence and into new areas of decision, in which the parents could not always be in control. The parents could also see how different their backgrounds were from Susan's. They began to realize that they could not necessarily expect quite the same behavior from Susan in today's world that had been demanded of them when they were teenagers. The family members seemed to emerge from the conversation with a better understanding of one another and a much deeper appreciation of the complex issues facing Susan at this time of her life.

THE TRABERTS

Elaine and Stuart came to see me about their teen-age son and daughter. The parents said that they simply did not know what was normal in adolescent behavior and what was not. Stuart felt confused about his role with the children at this point in their lives. Elaine still felt fairly close to her son, but said that she and her daughter were at loggerheads.

The parents stated that both the children performed well in school, for the most part, and that grades were not a worry. It was just that the family had always been close-knit and the children compliant, and now things had changed. Stuart said it was even difficult to like their daughter, now 14, since she seem unappreciative of whatever was done for her, hardly ever smiled, and spent much time alone in her room.

Their son, age 16, seemed to be on the go all the time. There were almost constant hassles with him regarding use of the family car, staying out on school nights, and not performing his chores around the house. Stuart essentially felt betrayed that his son, whom he had always regarded as a "really good kid," was behaving in such a manner.

From what the Traberts said, it seemed to me that they had two normally difficult and normally troublesome adolescent children, who were experiencing the natural turmoils and confusions of this period of life. I said this to the Traberts,

and I went on to explain more to them about the adolescent process. We talked about the formation of identity, the crisis of identity in adolescence, the Peter Pan complex, the displaced, irrational, anger toward parents, the half-baked logic system of the teenager, teen-age sex, and teen-age use of drugs. As we talked, both parents gained a better perspective on the ways of teenagers in general and decided that their children were not so bad after all.

I also pointed out some concepts and attitudes that might be useful to them in their relationship with their children. Primarily, I underlined ways of maintaining an emotional center, of providing benign reality confrontations, and of helping their adolescents develop better logical thinking.

The chapters that follow cover all the matters I discussed with the Traberts, detailing the various aspects of the developmental phase of life known as *adolescence*, and explaining how you as a parent may be of assistance to your own adolescents.

CHAPTER 3

Developing an Identity:
The Early Years

What is an identity anyway? How do you get one?
Question to a psychologist after his lecture

Many people have heard or read about something called the "adolescent identity crisis."

If you are the parent of a teen-age child, you undoubtedly will agree that some sort of crisis occurs during adolescence. But, like most parents, you probably don't know much about the nature of the crisis. Or what to do about it. Or if anything can or even should be done about it. Or what an identity is, anyway.

The ideas and feelings that we have about ourselves make up our *identity*. These feelings come from what we think about ourselves and from what we think *others* think about us, When these ideas about ourselves become fairly set and stable, we feel as though we know who we are. We know our role in life reasonably well, and we're fairly sure of our values and judgments. We have an *identity*.

Many child specialists believe that the process of forming an identity begins at birth. Some even believe that our personality is influenced by whether our birth was easy or difficult. In any case, identity formation starts very early in life.

The way infants and young children are treated by others begins to shape their feelings about themselves. Reciprocally, people's treatment of them is influenced by the way children act. For example, some babies seem to have naturally "easy"

ways, or "sweet dispositions." Others are cranky, have colic, and cry a lot for no obvious reasons. The adults in their lives are likely to respond one way to babies who gurgle and coo, and another way to babies who fuss all the time. You might expect that the baby with the easy disposition, who's no trouble at all, has the advantage. Sometimes, but not always. For instance, if there is another child in the family who is difficult to raise, that child might get the lion's share of Mommy's attention, leaving the easy baby in need of more cuddling and reassurance.

So you can't necessarily predict which kind of child will get "better" responses from the adults. But certainly the basic disposition of the infant and young child does influence how the adults respond.

The point is that events and people shape the child, and the child also shapes events and people. This is the way that an identity is gradually hammered out. Some experts feel that by as early as the age of 3 or 4 the child has a basic feeling of who he or she is, of self-worth or lack of it, and of how he or she fits into the world. The main influences during this phase are the parents. Siblings, nurses, and others who are part of or closely involved with the family, such as grandparents or other relatives, can also be influential, depending upon how much or how little they interact with the young child.

During this early phase of identity formation, the child has the task of eventually figuring out that the world "out there," beyond oneself, is something different from oneself. Another very important thing that the young child must begin to realize is that the whole world does not revolve around him or her.

Perhaps this realization of being just part of the big world, not the center of it, is the first true identity crisis a child faces. Child guidance professionals often see young children who are having severe anxieties about being separated from mother when left with baby-sitters. These anxious feelings seem to be the child's way of protesting the loss of mother's undiluted attention.

Just a few years after the young child has become more or less accustomed to the idea that there are others in the family and the world, another potential identity crisis looms on the horizon. This one involves going off to school.

School, be it nursery school or kindergarten, represents a first major step outside of the confines and protection of family and home. At home children are likely to be considered very special, with much said about their every drawing or other clever actions. But probably not at school. Now they must compete for teacher's attention. And the competition does not involve just a brother or sister or two. It involves 25 or 30 other kids! And each child is not only trying for teacher's attention, but also trying to learn such demanding skills as "making friends," "being a good sport," "being a good listener," "being a good sharer," and the like.

So by school time, life can get awfully complicated. It is no surprise then that the early school years, for many children, constitute a kind of identity crisis. Their roles are changing. They are having to move from early childhood within the family to interactions and adjustments outside of the family. At the same time that these complex social learning adjustments are taking place, the child also has to begin learning things such as reading, writing, and arithmetic. School is ready for all children who are age 5 or 6. But because of the uneven nature of physical and psychological development, not all children are ready for school at this age.

We adults rarely think of the first few years of school as a time of identity crisis for children. We tend to think of it as an "adjustment period." But whatever we call it, big changes take place in the early school years. When children are reasonably adequate intellectually and emotionally and also school-ready from a developmental standpoint, they will generally adjust to teachers and classmates and move on through the elementary school years without too much difficulty. The process is not particularly complicated by physical changes in children at this age, since their growth involves more or less gradual changes in height and weight.

In this way children spend the first 10 or 11 years of life in our culture: first, getting used to the idea that they aren't the center of anyone's universe, not even Mother's and Father's; then, getting used to leaving whatever comforts and safeties home may offer and going out into the world of teachers, classmates, books, rules, and time demands. During all this, they are also being molded by hundreds of thousands of interactions with others around them.

At the end of 10 to 12 years, they have developed a much stronger and more well-defined sense of self. They may or may not like themselves. They may feel confident in some areas and not in others. They may be poor students but good athletes or vice versa. They may or may not have mastered the fine art of making friends or getting along with adults. But no matter what, for good or bad, they have some idea about themselves and about the world around them. They have basic identities.

Then puberty hits and everything changes. The change is quick, drastic, and irrevocable. It can be for better or for worse. Almost always, the changes are very disturbing, disruptive, and confusing.

CHAPTER 4

Identity Crisis: The Teen Years

Can you tell me if this is normal? I was just sitting in my room one day. I realized that I didn't know who I was. I looked in the mirror and saw a stranger. Who is that? I felt a sadness and I began to cry. I felt that the *me* was gone and I didn't know how to get me back or even who me was. Is that normal?

A 14-year-old boy's question to me

I don't know my son anymore. He is not the person whom I have loved and lived with for the past thirteen years. I guess it's just "adolescent craziness" but I hate it. He is moody and withdrawn. He doesn't spend time with the family and just stays in his room a lot. He seems to be neither happy nor unhappy. He is just so different from what he used to be.

Comments from a mother

I know who the hell I am. I'm the captain of the football team.

A 15-year-old boy

A dolescence is as important for identity formation as all the years of childhood that came before. This is so even though a person's identity does begin to take shape during the early years of life.

It is not that the early years suddenly don't count when the child reaches puberty. But at puberty and throughout adolescence, the character development that has taken place

during childhood is melted down and reformed in the pressure cooker of a few years of quick and intense changes. The result of these changes consists of a mixture of the childhood personality traits and the new ingredients arising from what happens, or does not happen, to the young person in the teen years.

I have seen bright and secure children reach puberty only to be betrayed by their own pituitary glands, which provide them with no growth spurt equivalent to that of their peers. This creates much inner anguish. Other youngsters feel left out socially. Some perceive themselves as less attractive or less bright than their peers. Some must deal with parents who feel threatened and perhaps overreact in some way to the changes in size and physical development of their child.

In adolescence a great deal happens very quickly. There is often a feeling of loss of control, a feeling sometimes shared by both teens and their parents. Almost always, there is some degree of psychological pain, confusion, and general unhappiness at one time or another and for one reason or another.

Psychological pain is as real as physical pain, and such feelings must be dealt with in some way. Teenagers, like all of us, use various defense mechanisms. Many young people use withdrawal as a major defense against feelings of anxiety, confusion, turbulence, and unrest. In the simplest form, they may withdraw into their rooms, their daydreams, or into themselves. They may shut themselves off from others, especially their own parents. Up to a point, of course, all this is normal and expected for this age.

However, if their inner feelings of storm and stress become more intense, teenagers may withdraw by dropping out of school or running away from home, or by retreating into a more serious emotional disturbance such as schizophrenia.

Another major form of emotional pullback seen among young people today is involvement with drugs. Drug use is very frightening to most parents and rightly so. If you know or strongly suspect your child is drug-involved, you may want to turn directly to Chapter 12 on drugs.

The ultimate form of withdrawal for any person is suicide. Suicide among teenagers is on the rise. An average of 13 teenagers kill themselves each day in the United States, a total that approaches 5,000 per year. Dr. Michael Peck of the Los Angeles Suicide Prevention Center states, "Before 1965, the suicide rate increased with age, beginning in the mid 60s. Today it increases rapidly in the teen years, peaks at 20, then goes up again in the [later years]." Some professionals consider adolescence to be "suicideogenic," because of the rate of psychological and physical changes occurring then and because of the general lack of support from parents, schools, and the adult community at large.

Some teenagers react to their confusion and turmoil by spilling out their feelings through actions. These youngsters are often rebellious and resistant to all authority. They are, in effect, trouble waiting to happen. They often are physically violent to each other or to anyone who crosses their path. The mindless violence of the so-called Punk Rockers or New Wave movements provides extreme examples of acting-out behavior with group sanction. These young people are indulging in self- and peer-glorification with group identity and acceptance. Their outward violence toward themselves and others seems to reflect their own inner turbulence.

The following statement by a 17-year-old boy illustrates the odd feelings and depth of bewilderment that can come upon a deeply troubled youth.

> Sometimes I look in the bathroom mirror and I don't see anyone there at all. Yet, there are voices whispering and telling me that I don't know what happened to me in the past but they do, and that I don't know where I really am but they do. They also tell me that I can't figure out who I am without their help. I look and listen and wait, but I still haven't got their help and I still don't know who I am.

This boy was subsequently diagnosed as schizophrenic. On the other hand, some children go into and through

their teen-age years quite well, even when you might not expect they would. For example, I have seen children, whose first 10 or 11 years of life was nightmarish, emerge on the other side of adolescence strong and sure of themselves. The experience of the teen years was *positive* for them, perhaps because of fortunate physical development, or the discovery of a talent or a special ability to cope. This positive experience apparently helped them to overcome the problems of their early years and go on to develop a strong, positive identity. Tom is a good example.

When Tom was 8 years old his parents divorced. The marriage had never been good and Tom had witnessed many arguments, including his father's striking his mother. Nonetheless, through these years Tom and his father had been inseparable. Tom remembers that he "worshipped the ground" his father walked on.

Tom's father remarried about a year after the divorce and started a new family. After the baby was born, Tom's father came to visit him less and less. Soon the father no longer visited him at all. Tom had apparently been replaced by the new baby. He occasionally sought out his father by visiting his office after school, but his father made it clear that he no longer was concerned about him.

Gradually Tom sank into a deep depression. The depression apparently consisted of many angry feelings Tom had for his father, which he could not express directly. He developed many compulsive behaviors, such as hoarding the sports section of newspapers, wearing the same clothes day after day, and collecting thousands of used soft drink cans.

Although psychotherapy seemed somewhat useful to Tom in terms of helping him understand and deal with his father's actions, it was not until he reached puberty and began to grow taller and stronger that much greater personality changes began to be seen. In Tom's early teens he became attracted to running and began to channel his energies in that direction. He was strong, powerful, and very fast. In a short time he was winning awards in school track competitions. His grades

improved. He began to make a life for himself and compensate for the deep feelings of rejection and anger he had experienced as a child.

This is not to say, of course, that changes in puberty always resolve problems created in childhood. But in Tom's case, his athletic success in the early teens enabled him to regain much of the self-confidence and self-respect that had been lost when his father rejected him. Nothing can change the past, but some things help ease the wounds of the past. With continued counseling, Tom now realizes that his father's rejection of him had little to do with him personally. The father obviously had his own problems. Tom can now discuss his hurt and pain; he no longer has to hold the feelings inside. He has positive feelings about himself. His own hard work and the fortunate physical changes at puberty have provided him with strength, speed, self-esteem, and peer acceptance.

We saw in Chapter 3 that one of the main tasks of the infant and young child is to gain an identity. We saw that this sense of identity develops out of the child's experiences and attempts to make sense out of things that happen, as well as the way parents, peers, and others react to his personality.

The process of human development includes not only gains, but elements of loss as well. The child, in order to become more and more his or her own person, must increasingly separate from mother and overcome the dependency of infancy and early childhood. Now, in adolescence, we see a similar process of separation and increasing individuality. In the teens, the young person must separate from *both* parents. This is a normal process that eventually leads to becoming an independent adult. Parents often don't understand that this breaking away is typical and necessary in adolescent development. They fear that they are losing their children, and they sometimes try to hold on tightly. Such parental holding-on often leads to much friction and many problems between parents and teenager.

> I see myself in my daughter. It totally frightens me. She
> seems so vulnerable and frail, as I was as a teenager. I
> see her feelings hurt. I worry about her drug use and if
> she is into sex too much. I know I have to let go, let her
> become her own person. But I'm just plain scared. I
> don't even know of what. Of her failing, I guess, of her
> screwing up in some way and once more being hurt. I
> want to help but she won't really let me into her
> thoughts anymore. Besides, I even know that I'm not
> good for her when I'm this way. I think my anxieties
> flow over on her. And I think she resents this, my put-
> ting my fears about her onto her.

There are also other ways in which the developing teenager
has a more difficult and complicated task than the infant or
young child. Although children gradually lose a sense of
oneness with mother and father, they do remain within the
fold of warm and reassuring parental protection. Being small
and having little decision-making power in the family, they
more or less do as they are told by adults or by older and
more powerful siblings or peers. Generally, little is expected
of them in terms of competency and responsibility, and often
much love and affection are lavished upon them by parents.
They may even feel a rather exaggerated sense of self-
importance, especially if reared in a child-centered home.

For the teenager it is an altogether different story! As they
go about the difficult task of becoming separate from parents,
more tends to be expected, even demanded, both at home
and at school. New peer pressures loom. The first glimmers
of the frightening vision of ultimately leaving home base and
"being on your own" begins to flash into consciousness.
Then, just as the world begins to make these increased and
more complex demands, the young person starts to change
bodily, mentally, and emotionally.

An attractive, intelligent high school girl who had become
school phobic expressed her fears this way:

> It's really weird. I can just get scared for no reason at all.
> If I'm with someone, it helps. But, if I have to go up to a

group of strangers or eat lunch by myself or go into a
new classroom, I just freak! I think everyone is looking
at me and wondering about me. When I get these feelings I just want to be home in my room. Its safe there.
My parents are safe. They take care of me. Yet, I know
that I've got to take care of myself. Be "on my own,"
whatever that means.

Whether youngsters develop a positive or negative self-
concept in the years before puberty, one thing is certain—
identity or self-concept will change in various important
ways during the adolescent years. At this time, the youngster
embarks upon the process of the disintegration of a relatively
stable and familiar childhood identity. At the same time,
parts of that former identity must be reintegrated with the
various new aspects of the person gradually evolving.

This dual process of tearing down the old familiar self and
rebuilding it into a new self is a central theme in adolescence.
You can easily see the potential for a great deal of pain and
confusion. As the young adolescent "loses" child identity
(former self), the only identity known since birth, the new
and urgent transformation crowds in. Facial and other bodily
features are changing. Sexual energies and desires are literally
flowing, and these interests and feelings can no longer be
ignored. Thus, various changes in personality, intellect, and
social status are suddenly thrust upon the young person.
These changes are unavoidable. They cannot be put off or
denied. The teenager must come to grips with them one way
or another.

Unfortunately our society offers few if any legitimate rites
of passage from childhood to adulthood. For example, a
young man cannot go hunting and kill a lion, thereby gaining
admittance to the circle of young warriors, admittance to
"adulthood." It seems a loss and a confusion that we have not
created ways for our young to "prove" themselves and thus
gain easier and fuller acceptance in the eyes of society and in
their own eyes as they travel upward on the rungs of the
maturity ladder.

In the past, the Jewish custom of the Bar Mitzvah at age 13 rather formally recognized some of the major developmental and social status changes of young people. Now, however, this ritual seems to have little real meaning. California teenagers, at least, know that the *real* recognition of semi-adult status comes officially at age 16, the age at which one can obtain a driver's license—a sort of "Car Mitzvah."

Perhaps you have forgotten the pain and the "weird feelings" of your own adolescence. Repression is a good defense sometimes. But if you do not remember your teen-age confusions, or if luckily you had few traumas or problems during that time of life, you may not be in the best position to assist your young person.

However, perhaps you can empathize with your adolescent's situation, given a moment's reflection. Imagine the strange feelings you might have if the *who* you had been (as a child) was beginning to slip away slowly but surely. Further, imagine that some sort of new "who" was emerging, a who of more complex and powerful moods and drives, but a who of considerable unsureness and worry about one's self in the world.

An adult experience similar to this is provided in Franz Kafka's short story, *The Metamorphosis.* A man awakens one morning to find that he has, overnight, changed into a large bug. The bug-person is faced not only with the problem of learning how to roll over off his back, but he must attempt to communicate with family members, who are shouting at him through the door in human language. He has to deal with his deep feelings of shame and guilt over the inexplicable change that has come over him. And he must try to handle the terrible anxiety created by the problems inherent in his changed status, shape, and function.

This story is only the product of a novelist's powerful imagination. But consider your own adult anxieties and unease at changing jobs, moving to a new neighborhood, or getting a divorce. To some extent, each of these changes involves part of your own "identity." As you move from one

life situation—job, neighborhood, spouse—to another, your sense of yourself, your *identity*, is altered to some degree. You may no longer be Mr. or Mrs. Doe, insurance salesperson, but rather, Mr. or Mrs. Doe, small business owner. Or you might have become someone's "ex-spouse" or "former New Yorker." Or moved from "employed" to "unemployed."

The coping behaviors that you had found to be more or less effective in your previous job, neighborhood, or relationships might or might not be effective in the new situation. You probably recognize this possibility. And perhaps you are sometimes uneasy about new experiences, at least until you see whether or not your old patterns of behavior can be used effectively in the new environment or relationship. To the extent that you can adapt your previous coping methods to the new situation, you see yourself as having dealt with it adequately, and your uneasiness tends to abate.

But teenagers have little experience that they can refer to for successful methods of coping with various new situations. One exception to this might be their academic performance. Generally, skills such as studying or paying attention in class, which worked well in the elementary grades, will still be effective in high school. Other factors, however, can arise to neutralize the use of these skills. For example, they might find themselves disinterested and/or rebellious, or perhaps be faced by even more profound emotional difficulties interfering with their success.

As the young person reaches adolescence, then, the only prior "training" experienced was in being a child. And while it is obvious that what we learn during childhood about ourselves, others, and the things of this world is clearly very important, these experiences only partially equip us for the passage through the teens.

No longer do the childhood rules apply. The youngster no longer even looks like a child and is less willing to let adults exercise large amounts of control. At the same time, the youngster is increasingly thrust into social situations (often involving drugs, sex, or antisocial behavior) in which impor-

tant and difficult decisions must quickly be made, usually without benefit of parental direction or discussion.

Whatever the youngster has developed as identity over the first decade or so of life begins to go through such drastic changes that it is of little or no help in dealing with many of the new pressures and situations encountered.

With the partial disintegration of childhood identity comes the beginnings of reintegration toward adult identity. This new integration comes from the teenager's initial steps in dealing with various new concepts and feelings. These new concepts include, for instance, the change in self-perception from a physical standpoint. It includes major changes in social standing with both adults and peers. New expectations and responsibilities, from others and oneself, are felt, as is the increasing internal drive for independence from parents.

A dramatic example of a change in self-perception due to physical changes is seen in the statement of a star high school basketball player who, with the aid of motivation, glands, and barbells, effected an astonishing change in muscular development in the period of time between his eleventh-grade season and his senior year.

> I worked out three to four times a week (with weights). I ate like crazy. I just didn't want to be pushed around under the basket anymore. I didn't want to be called chicken ever again. When my senior year started, I remember getting slammed against the wall by some big guy from Dorsey (High School). I slammed back, and the dude went down. I got kicked out of the game, but it was really worth it. That night I looked into the mirror in the bathroom and saw what the other dudes were seeing—one tough, mean, big sumbitch. I wasn't going to take anything from anybody anymore.

The teenager's move toward independence from parents and other adults appears to be mainly due to increased feelings of personal power (physical and intellectual), combined with the more or less natural tendency to throw off adult authority anyway.

This increased independence is not without emotional cost. For one thing, it often must be won in various types of confrontation with parents or other adults. For another thing, becoming *independent* clearly implies that one is no longer *dependent*. Yet, being dependent still has definite attractions.

As the youngster moves into the early teens, the dependency-independence conflict rages back and forth across the emotional landscape. The powerful magnet of childhood dependency competes with the attractions of increased independence of thought and action, and independence is likely to be perceived as a mixed blessing. Being more independent implies the assumption of responsibilities that have previously been handled by parents for the most part.

Even the word *responsibility* seems to hold negative meanings for many teenagers. A 16-year-old said:

> That is the most hated word—responsibility. I've always got to be responsible for myself or for something or other. I have to prove myself *responsible* at school, at home. To hell with responsible. I don't want it. Responsibility sucks.

This type of reaction is typical of many teenagers. Even so, the general task of adolescence includes becoming willing and able to take more responsibility for one's actions or inactions.

As a further part of identity reintegration, the early- and middle-adolescent tends to reassess various relationships with others, including relationships with parents and oneself. There is a great need to assess oneself, to examine and evaluate feelings and a changing appearance. This need is often perceived by adults as narcissistic selfishness or, in kinder terms, self-centeredness. But when you look at this narcissism as part of the teenager's struggle to learn more about who and what he or she is, it is more understandable. Indeed, great amounts of self-exploration are necessary for identity reintegration to take place. One teen-age girl wrote the following:

I spend a lot of time looking in the mirror, not because I'm vain. It's just that I'm interested in altering things that can be altered. It [looking in the mirror] also lets me become more comfortable with how I look, to myself and to other people. I like to know what I look like when I'm making certain statements or when I make a face. When I was in junior high, I would never even look in a neon-lit mirror such as a bathroom mirror. Consequently, I would endure the pain until I got home and could be in a bathroom with soft, muted lighting. It's only been in the past few years that I've begun to look at myself in a different light—if you'll excuse the pun.

The teenagers' relationships with peers also change as they move from the rather loose and easy childhood of playing together to the much more complicated and subtle social interactions of adolescence. Peer relationships gradually begin to take precedence over parental relationships and parental authority. And this becomes a source of much friction in many households.

A father of three teenagers somewhat wistfully states:

We [the family] used to do a lot of things together. Camping, Disneyland, trips to San Francisco, and so on. Now, it seems, my wife and I go one way and they [the teenagers] go another. All they seem to be interested in is their friends and who is doing what with whom and when. They sure aren't interested in us. I guess that's normal. But it does seem as if something is lost for all of us.

The importance of these peer relationships cannot be underestimated. We derive much of our feelings of self-esteem, our positive or negative identities, from the reactions of others to us. And in adolescence, it is mainly the young person's relationships with peers that influence feelings about self. This is a major shift in the source of self-esteem and a very powerful force. In early years one may have received good feelings about oneself from adults. But if one experiences

dismal social failure in high school, this can simply wipe out earlier self-confidence and self-liking. To be liked by the other young people may become one of the most important goals in life during this time.

A popular teen-age boy states:

> You can't be too different or you're out. You have to be cool, but not too cool. One of the hardest things is to 'put down' [not smoke marijuana]. Sharing a doobie is a way of making a friend, of being part of things. The bong [marijuana pipe] is sort of like the peace pipes used by the Indians.

In other words, you've got to go along to get along. In some things, such as conformity in slang or clothes, going along seems harmless. In other things (for example drugs or sex or violence), going along can create some very large problems for the young person and the family.

If a teenager does succeed with peers, it can sometimes wipe out earlier disappointments and impart a new sense of self-confidence and self-acceptance. In many instances, the teenager's need to conform to peers and be accepted is so powerful that only lip service will be paid to the adults who still control many of the good or important things of life, such as money, cars, grades, and jobs.

> I don't argue with my folks much [one teenager says]. I just say "fine" to whatever they say and then go do my own thing anyway. What're they going to do? Beat me? If they did, I'd split. Besides, what they don't know doesn't hurt them. If my parents ever knew all the crap that goes on [with teenagers], they'd freak out. It's easy to shine [put something over on; not pay attention to] most adults. I go the easy way.
>
> [One especially articulate teenager notes]: "From eighth grade on all I thought about was what others [peers] might be thinking about me. I really needed to be part of things, to feel accepted. Sometimes I felt I was in, sometimes not—and I was going with the right peo-

ple. I can only imagine the horror suffered by the out kids, the straight kids. If I had to smoke a J to be in, I'd smoke a J; if I had to screw, I'd screw; whatever. It just didn't matter at that moment what my parents had taught me, wanted for me. I *had* to be accepted by the other kids."

Another bright boy, Fred, never learned how to gain peer acceptance. Now a physics major at a major local university, he says, "I was horny. I wanted a girl. I wanted friends. I even joined the Sci-Fi Club in high school so I could meet someone, anyone, guys or girls. I don't know what was the matter. The harder I tried, the more others turned away. I was a lonely bastard. My parents were no help. Always after me to make friends, and to get straight As. They totally confused things for me. Now, years later, I've finally learned how to relax and try to find people in common interest groups. I still don't feel relaxed socially or sexually. Maybe I never will."

During all of this struggle, a process of *internalization of identity* is taking place. This means, first, that the teenager is taking in, sifting, and sorting all feelings about OKness or not-OKness as a person. While the major source of feelings comes from the degree of acceptance and approval by friends, this can be reinforced by other things of value discovered about oneself, such as talent for playing the guitar or being a lab assistant, or for getting good grades. Other young people and even adults also influence thoughts of identity. (Perhaps you can remember the influence of a favorite teacher whose approval was important to you, after whom you may have tried to pattern yourself.) Movie stars and rock stars are important, as are athletes and other glamorous heroes in the public eye. For some adolescents, antiheroes such as Hell's Angels may become important influences.

No matter what kinds of models the teenager has chosen, the value placed on them nearly always depends on whether they augment popularity with friends.

As the young person takes in all the input from the world, internalizes it and accepts it as authentic and real, certain

standards and feelings of identity develop. They become yardsticks for evaluating actions, making decisions, and judging right and wrong or appropriateness and inappropriateness. The face in the mirror is recognized and accepted. A sense of identity is reformed and established.

This process of identity disintegration and reintegration is probably never entirely completed. As long as we live, changes continue to take place inside us. We constantly assess our past, present, and future, more intensely at some ages than at others. *But at no time in our lives will we ever again face such a drastic reorganization of both our physical and our psychological selves as in the early years of adolescence.*

What, if anything, can you as a parent and/or concerned adult do to help your youngster through the changes and confusions of this time of life? More specifically, what might you do to assist in the search for identity, which is the urgent and primary task?

I have said that if you understand how something works you are better off than if you are ignorant of what is going on. A balky engine can drive you up the wall with frustration if you don't know how to fix it. A little knowledge can help you adjust the engine to run smoothly.

In like manner, if you comprehend, even rather generally, the nature of the adolescent transition period, your behavior in the face of the anxiety, confusion, surliness, and disconcerting behavior of your teenager can be toned down and steadied. You can nurture, understand, and provide structure to a young person who may be feeling alienated, misunderstood, and highly confused. You can also retain your own sanity!

But you must clearly understand that no matter what you do, no matter how skilled and gifted you may be, this does not automatically "cure" adolescence. You cannot rid the young person of all confusions, irrational resentments, and general difficulties in finding identity. But your *adult steadiness* is useful and provides stability. Your calmness in

the face of erratic and unreasonable behavior tends to have a calming effect. It is not helpful when chaos and confusion are reflected by responsible adults.

If an adult is sick, the anxiety level increases markedly if the doctor is also confused and anxious. You need your doctor to offer the demeanor of calmness and of being in control. This helps you. So it is with young people. They need you and the other adults with whom they deal to present a calm, reasoned, and structured viewpoint in the face of their own inner lack of calmness, structure, and rationality.

How is it possible to do this? For example, how do you stay calm and rational when your teenager appears to be flying apart with anger or despair or rebellion? How do you hold the line against the enormous and irrational pressures exerted on you by a teenager who absolutely insists on doing what you absolutely forbid? How do you cope with epithets and street language when they are being thrown at you? In other words, how do you keep from going up the wall? And how do you keep yourself from becoming heavy-handed or trying to "get even"?

It certainly isn't easy, but it can be done. I have seen thousands of parents struggle through it, some of them with more success than they had thought possible. I have been through it with my own children and survived so far. I believe you can do it too.

This book contains several how-to-do-it chapters. They have such titles as "Handling the Anger of the Adolescent," "Defining Tolerance Limits," and "Spending Quality Time Together." They offer specific suggestions for meeting the everyday kinds of difficulties that you face with your teenager. They suggest how to be as helpful as possible with your young person, while also saving yourself.

If you are feeling besieged and need some immediate "instructions," go ahead and read the how-to chapters (numbers 14 through 19). They will make sense to you now, and I believe they will be helpful. And they will make even more sense and be more helpful once you have read all the

chapters leading up to them and you understand such ideas as the adolescent as Peter Pan, the fear of responsibility, the meaning of work and money, and what drugs are all about.

I would like to complete this chapter by talking in a general way about (1) meeting your teenager's irrationality and anger with calmness and reason; (2) holding a stable and "centered" emotional position; and (3) maintaining an underlying belief that your young person will, with time, resolve the issues of identity and move on toward becoming a separate person.

You need not be afraid to say no or to offer a strong structure for your early-adolescent (puberty to, say, 14 or 15). Strong, positive structure seems very useful to a young person who is coming unglued and may be quite destabilized psychologically. By mid-adolescence, however, you should begin turning over to your teenager more and more responsibility for behavior and the consequences of that behavior.

In a letter published in the *Los Angeles Times*, a 16-year-old high school girl expresses the great, if sometimes unfounded, despair felt by teenagers struggling to understand themselves and their place in today's world. After pondering the identity of her generation, she concludes that they are lost, overwhelmed by the complex and perplexing realities of life. She sees herself and others her age fleeing from forces and events that seem to control their lives. But she strikes a hopeful note with her wish that the running away and hiding will stop and that young people who share her desire to improve the world will begin seeking ways to make it a less frightening and frustrating place.

I listen and I accept such comments from teenagers. It seems poor strategy to argue the point that other times and other places have also perceived themselves as beleaguered and on the verge of obliteration. (The teenagers of Troy, perhaps? The young people of the concentration camp in Terezin?) Rather, it seems much more helpful to listen to the young and to accept their confusions, angers, and anguishes. It also seems helpful for them to receive one further gift from the adult—the *attitude* that young people will find a way and

will gradually make some sense out of life and come to feel reasonably good about their identity.

Of course the young writer of these eloquent words is lost. The world has "overwhelmed" her and others of her generation as the reality of what life is and is not all about begins to dawn. While the teen-age author is correct in stating that we are shaped by the things that happen to us in the world, the implication seems to be that in some way she and her generation are "lost" because of those events. You as an adult can recognize the confusions and stresses of the world, for they certainly are real. But at the same time you realize that much of the teenager's struggles and difficulties are taking place in an internal world, even if they appear to be imposed from outside.

You can be very influential with teenagers, though you may sometimes think otherwise. One way you can help is to be interested and pay attention when they act reasonable and mature. This helps to reinforce positive qualities of selfhood. Of course this assumes that you and your adolescent have a sufficiently good relationship so that you can talk to each other with reasonable civility. By the same token, you can help in curtailing some of the more negative aspects of childhood personality. It may help to recall that earlier behavior such as thumb-sucking, bed-wetting, tantrums, whining, and fighting with siblings usually has been outgrown as the young peron matured into adolescence. With help, the fragmentations and difficulties of the adolescent phase will also be outgrown. Greater personality integrations will gradually be seen. Young people will grow up.

You can also help both your teenager and yourself if you do not feel too threatened or hurt as your child begins to be much more interested in peer relationships than in you. Adolescence is a time for becoming an individual, for breaking away from parents, and you would be wise to encourage this process within limits. Obviously, what you should allow a 13-year-old to do in breaking away is far different from what you might encourage a 16-year-old to do.

There are many things you cannot and should not try to do for your teenager. For example, you cannot guarantee a good self-concept or academic, social and maturation success. You cannot give these assurances because you do not control all of the internal or external variables which shape life. But you can be extremely important in your teenager's development. In work, apprentice systems often teach most effectively. In life, we all need good, experienced, and kind guides to help us get started and keep going.

Many years ago, John Locke, the British philosopher, wrote these words about the needs of young people:

> Children are travellers newly arrived in a strange country, of which they know nothing; we should therefore make conscience not to mislead them. They are strangers to all we are acquainted with; and all the things they meet with are at first unknown to them, as they once were to us; and happy are they who meet with civil people that will comply with their ignorance and help them to get out of it.

Perhaps the best general advice I can offer to any parent, teacher, coach, or adult friend of any young person, is to strive to be a "civil person" as you offer assistance on the path toward adulthood. An important part of this is to demonstrate, in whatever ways you can, your conviction that you are dealing with a valuable person you believe will ultimately come through the struggles and find the way. For a frightened, upset, and emotionally unstable adolescent, your faith may be one of the most important ways you can help.

CHAPTER 5

Nobody Really Wants to Grow Up: The Adolescent as Peter Pan

Teen: My father is simply screwed. All he wants me to do is work, work, work. I *hate* doing work for him. Now he has me digging out a drain line down a back slope. He's a slave driver, man, a jerk. And he won't give me money or let me use the car unless I do this crap.

Counselor: What about your getting a job?

Teen: What? Regular work. That's too screwed to be considered. Day after day, go to work. Get paid peon wages. No way. Not for me. I won't do it. I'll never do it.

Counselor: It seems that you don't want to work for your dad and you don't want to work for yourself. Maybe you just don't feel ready for a commitment to a work schedule yet?

Teen: No, I want to work, sort of. I just wish I had lotsa bucks—megabucks—many dollars. But the old man won't give 'em. And, work. A regular job. That's lame man, lame. A regular job. Sounds like I'm a man or something.

Counselor: You did say last week or so that you ought to be considered a man now and your own boss. You said that no one had any hold on you and your parents ought to just let you do what you want to do.

Teen: That's right. They should. Why do they keep hassling me? Why don't they just let me alone? They have no *right* to tell me what to do.

Counselor: I guess they feel they have some right, maybe some duty, to try and guide your life in positive ways as best they can. You don't seriously think that your parents should just provide you with money or other support no matter what you do, do you?

Teen: No, not really, I guess. It's just that the old man is such a *worker*. I mean, he just seems to get off on work! What's so good about work, anyway? Why can't I just surf all day and party all night? That's what I want to do.

Excerpt from a counseling session

Let's face it, no one really wants to grow up. At least, if to be "grown up" means having to work regularly, be under pressure, pay bills, and generally hassle with the world. A young child has no choice but to put up with parents and teachers and others who lay down rules and regulations about such things as bedtime and homework. But the child also has the advantage of having others make decisions, of being able to rely on others for food, clothing, nice things to play with, and for safety and security.

The teenager, however, gradually begins to realize that everything is a trade-off. To get the increased freedom desired, increased *responsibility* (that hated word) must be demonstrated. To have independence, dependence must be given up. It is a tough choice, and part of the general task of adolescence is to work through that choice. This pull between independence and dependence, between the desire to remain a child and the desire to become an adult, is so difficult and complicated that it is no wonder it takes most of us many years, the teen years and beyond, to begin to resolve these issues.

It is quite understandable that a part of all of us wants to remain a child. Somewhere inside, each of us has a wish to remain in a childhood state of low pressures and responsibilities coupled with quick and easy gratification of our desires. Such

feelings are probably universal in the psychological makeup of human beings.

The adolescent stands midway between childhood and adulthood, strongly pulled in both directions, very reluctant to leave the garden of childhood, but really wanting to get on to the joys and rewards of being a separate person. A strong regressive need to hold on to childhood's security and safety is in sharp conflict with the need to progress toward increased freedom with responsibility: adulthood.

Society too, at this point in life, begins to exert more pressure for taking responsibility for one's own behavior. Even so, society does not quite expect complete responsibility. Our juvenile justice system, for example, does not hold an early- or middle-adolescent as fully accountable as an adult. As a society we seem to realize that there is a transition from childhood, a time of little accountability for one's actions, into adulthood and full accountability. There is a fuzzy area called "adolescence," in which one is not exactly a child, but yet not quite an adult.

James Barrie's lovely story, *Peter Pan*, seems to capture the essence of what we are talking about. Taken simply at face value, *Peter Pan* gives us a delightful picture of the wish of all children to be able somehow to continue forever as children, to have all sorts of adventures, and to have magical powers, such as the ability to fly, which would help one get out of any scrapes which might come along. But there is more to this story. On another level, Pan expresses not just the child's desire to remain a child, but also the adolescent's and the adult's desires to do the same. It touches that deep inner part of each of us that wants to retain or recapture the real and imagined pleasures and delights of childhood, especially its *freedom.*

But, freedom from what? Or freedom to do what?

It seems to me that this freedom, for an adolescent, has to do with not being told what and how and when to do things, as children are told. It also means freedom not yet to accept the mantle of cares, responsibilities, and decisions of

adulthood. For a few brief, turbulent, admittedly unstable years, the teenager is "free," floating between childhood and adulthood. Unanchored. Unbalanced. Unsure and insecure. But free, even though this freedom creates further instabilities and anxieties. For freedom implies choices. Choices imply thinking. Thinking implies the realization of time past, time present, and time future.

Another way of expressing the young person's journey toward adulthood is to picture a traveler leaving the green pastures of a land well-known, a land of reasonable security, low pressures in terms of life decisions, and fairly high structure from parents and schools. Up to now the young person has lived in this realm of childhood. Now, however, the unseen and little understood pressures of natural development, and the societal changes that occur as we grow older, impose a forced exile from this land of security. A new land, the realm of adulthood, must be discovered.

From parents and others who already reside in adulthood, the word reaches the adolescent traveler that all is not serene and secure in the new land. Times are hard. One must do something called "work" which uses up time, is not always pleasant, and must be done more or less consistently. Also, one must think about something called "saving money" as well as such things as "buying a house," "paying for car insurance," and so on.

It is no wonder, then, that the teenager is a reluctant traveler and is not overly enthusiastic about the journey from child land to adult land. The adult world often looks awesome to the teenager and may seem hard and cold by comparison with the easy, dependent existence in child land.

From this viewpoint, you can begin to understand the surliness you may see in your own teenager, and the general resentment or outright rebellion against authority figures. It is true that one reason for rebellious, antisocial attitudes is that the teenager is testing limits, feeling oats, and more or less exploring for self-identity vis-a-vis his parents and other adults who have run life up to this point. But another reason

runs beneath this. At a subconscious level, a level which few teenagers or adults could verbally label, the adolescent is reluctant to leave the easy, green gardens of child land. There is a deep, unconscious resentment over being kicked out of a good place. In some strange way, events are being orchestrated to take away the joys of a relatively pressure-free childhood and impose the clearly pressure-laden existence of adulthood.

The teenager's resentful feelings are difficult for most of us to comprehend. We reason that we are trying to be nice people, we want the best for our children, we buy clothes and cars for them and send them on the best vacations we can afford. Why, then, are they so surly and unpleasant to us so often?

Well, if you (unconsciously) felt that you were losing something of great value, something you would have only once in your entire life, you might have deep feelings of confusion and anger. Not only is this loss fundamental and irrevocable, but you realize that you must now proceed into frightening and confusing new channels in life as you move toward the uncertainties of who and what you are to become in the future.

Teenagers sense the loss of their childhood days. They perceive the irrevocable surge forward of growth and development. The feeling that someday soon they must break away from parents and be on their own lurks beneath the surface of consciousness. The feeling is partly frightening, partly exhilarating, but always unsettling.

Teenagers, like all of us, tend to want to blame someone for their loss (of childhood) and for the forces that move them toward increased responsibility. Thus, much irrational resentment is directed at parents and other adults close to them. These irrational feelings are unsettling to parents, but they are, from a psychological standpoint, quite understandable.

Let's explore further the analogy of the adolescent as Peter Pan. You will recall that in Never-Never Land there were no

parents to direct or otherwise "bother" the young boys, the children whom Peter led. Nonetheless, the underlying need for parenting was expressed by Peter's seeking out the kindly Wendy to come and "mother" them all.

Captain Hook provides the exquisite, ominous sense of threat which human beings, in their vulnerability, tend to project into the world around them and must deal with by what psychologists call "coping mechanisms."

Peter Pan and his cronies, with the help of Wendy as mother figure and Tinker Bell as the "magical assistant" most of us long for, may be said to serve as a reasonably good example of arrested development, which all of us, if we could admit it honestly, really want in our own lives. Peter Pan, then, symbolizes our deep regressive wishes for freedom without responsibility. It is virtually a total denial that there is a more complicated developmental stage to which we must move as part of our effort to achieve higher levels of emotional maturity.

Peter might be said to represent "pleasure." What happens when, in real life, the child becomes the adolescent and pleasure collides with reality?

The slow but inevitable confrontation between pleasure and reality is rooted in infancy and childhood. Freud posed the infant as an example of "primary narcissism," meaning that the infant embodies the so-called pleasure principle. That is, the infant and young child are characterized by the "I want what I want when I want it" point of view, a view which Freud and other psychological thinkers gradually came to see as a part of all of us—the instinctual urge for immediate gratification of our desires.

Reality principles, on the other hand, represent the demands of others, the compromises and accommodations each must make to each if we are to live together, and the coming to terms with the demands of the external environment.

For Freud, then, one of the basic tasks of childhood, indeed of life itself, is the gradual process of adjusting the extreme, narcissistic desires of the selfish, self-centered infant/child

personality structure (conceived of as a part of each of us) to the powerful, reality-oriented demands placed upon each of us by the environment, an environment that houses parents, peers, teachers, and self.

Earlier we talked about how infants must adjust to the gradual realization that the world does not revolve around them. Continuing adjustments are demanded throughout childhood, especially upon entering school.

As in so much of life, lessons learned or battles fought at one level often must be learned or fought at other levels as life goes on. Regardless of how well the child resolves pleasure-reality confrontations, in adolescence the problem must be confronted once more, and it is much more intense and complex. As is true for the child, the teenager's resolution of this problem is crucial to later adult personality formation.

If a reasonable compromise of the pleasure-reality conflict has not been made by the time the young person reaches adolescence, adjustment at the adolescent level will be much more difficult and there will be the strong likelihood of personality disturbances.

Let's be clear in our language. By "pleasure" I mean quick and easy gratification, minimal care and concern for the needs and desires of others, little responsibility for personal actions, narcissism, and a general sense that others will provide gratification, sacrifice their own desires, and assume all responsibilities.

By "reality" I mean the demands of others, aspects of the environment, such as a door that will not open, and interactions with others, such as parents who sometimes say no. Of course, as the child becomes a teenager these reality demands are increasingly made by parents, teachers, and other authority figures, as well as by peers. Reality demands also tend to be developed from the inside, as the adolescent internalizes certain standards, drives, demands, and general self-directives.

Remember too that this rather complex pleasure versus reality conflict is taking place in the teenager at the same time that a great many other influences are emerging.

While professing strong demands for more freedom and independence (usually from parents), most adolescents may be seen as individuals who are being dragged kicking and screaming by unavoidable processes into a world of increasing demands, including pressures to make decisions in major areas such as drug use, educational direction, sex, and financial matters.

These realities can seem overwhelming to the young person who has depended upon others to make decisions. While there may be rebellion over being controlled by others, there is also comfort in the reassurance such dependency provides. Parents have been like demigods whose decisions somehow were always "right."

But as difficult as reality may seem, the adolescent cannot, and usually will not, rely heavily on adults, or accept their judgment or influence. Once again, there are gains and losses. By running things the adolescent has gained a certain amount of freedom. But there are significant losses as well. One of these is the fading of the illusion that parents are omnipotent. And this heightens awareness of one's own vulnerabilities while being thrust into the world of reality, ready or not, like it or not.

And many teenagers do not like it. They are resentful at a very deep level over the fact that they must grow up, stop being Peter Pan, and increasingly become more adult in their manner of meeting reality's demands. Such resentment is rarely verbalized. In fact, most teenagers are rarely even conscious of it. It is nonetheless there. And usually it has strong reverberations within the young person and within the relationship to parents and other authority figures.

So it is this deep, unspoken resentment about leaving the lush gardens of childhood and the freedom of Never-Never Land that causes so much of the friction between teenagers and adults. For the childish part of the adolescent personality still desires to be Peter Pan—to be able to play without having to pay and to continue to be taken care of and remain dependent.

To further compound the problem, the demigod parents are no longer seen as godlike. The child, who was vulnerable, physically weak, and ignorant of the ways of the world, needed to perceive parents as strong, protective, and virtually invulnerable and immortal. Upon entering adolescence, it is nearly too much for the child to come to terms with the fact that parents, those people who used to help, who in the early years solved difficulties and problems as if by magic, who offered structure and support, can no longer be of effective assistance in all, or even most, instances. The parent-gods have fallen. They were only mortals after all. And by inference realized only dimly and subconsciously, must not the adolescent too be only mortal, unlike the immortal Peter Pan?

All of these circumstances fuel an irrational, unreasoning, unverbalized, and unlabeled anger in the adolescent. The teenager's parents are closest to the situation and are therefore seen as the prime cause of problems. In some vague way they have failed in several important areas, while pressuring even more than before in others.

These feelings are not logical, of course, and this situation is not logical from the standpoint of objective reality. It is not even "fair" of the young person to expect parents to be perfect or expect them to be able to assist in all the complex interpersonal difficulties. Parents cannot furnish a sexual partner, guarantee social success, or be there to help make decisions in meeting pressures for drug use or sexual activity.

Unfortunately, a great many parents tend to misperceive the irrational part of their teenager's resentment and rebellion and look for logic when there is no logic—only feelings. They take the resentment personally. Then they overreact to their teenager's negative feelings with equally negative feelings. In such an atmosphere, the flash point often comes quickly and there are large and small emotional explosions of various sorts. Sometimes, of course, the parent's anger may be appropriate. That is, sometimes it is a reaction to something the young person has done. But more often it is simply a

misunderstanding of the nature of their adolescent's unhappiness, which the parent has taken too personally.

So when conflicts arise with your teenager, as they almost inevitably must, try to depersonalize them. Try to see that the anger really isn't meant for you. This is not easy to do. But remind yourself when your young person seems unfairly angry or rebellious that adolescence is a most difficult and complex stage of life. Not that you should passively permit resentments to be dumped on you, but you can keep yourself from overreacting to it. Your blowup in response to your teenager's anger creates a no-win situation. Anger usually generates more anger. And such mutual outbursts leave almost no one happy. Your tantrum or your own irrationality (such reasoning as "You can't go because I said so!"), does little to show your young person a better way of behaving.

You must also take care not to reinforce your teenager's negative or irrational behavior by deciding to give in rather than cause a blowup. This can be a large mistake. You may simply be proving that anger wins, that tantrums or threats to run away can prevail.

Instead of yielding to your natural desire to fight back when attacked, or to give in, you would do better to serve as an example of rational and reasonable behavior in the face of mood storms. Try to hold even, to state the contingencies under which a reasonable discussion might take place. You might say, for example, "When you calm down, we'll discuss the matter." You can also help by giving approving attention to your youngster for rational and reasonable behavior and for calming down after an outburst and in general behaving in a way that you would like to reinforce.

Irrational resentments are not the only possible source of friction between you and your teenager. Differences and misunderstandings can easily occur when your youngster overrates levels of maturity and competence. Teenagers sometimes tend to have misplaced confidence in themselves, even though subconsciously they are still quite uncertain about themselves.

At the same time, as a parent you may be underrating or minimizing your teenager's increasing maturity level. We parents are often quite unsure about whether or not we really want our children to grow up, since unconsciously we often understand that their growing up involves our own loss. First, of course, we lose the young person who moves away from home. This move is often seen by many parents as a loss of part of themselves. Second, when our *children* move out of our home the unavoidable implication is that they are now *adults*. This implication distinctly underlines the fact that we of the parent generation are growing older. Our own youth is lost!

These kinds of mixed feelings on the part of both parent and teenager are illustrated in the following summary of counseling notes. Both parties seemed to be sending many double messages.

> Sandy, a rather overprotected (by parents) high school girl, was urged by her counselor to seek an after-school job. Sandy was initially frightened by the prospect, but she perceived the need for such a move toward independence and saw it as the beginning of learning how to "get along in the world." At first, Sandy's parents were all for the idea, while Sandy seemed steeped in ambivalence and self-doubts.
>
> When Sandy began more serious job-seeking, however, her parents began to undermine various employment possibilities. They raised first one objection, then another.
>
> Finally, Sandy and her parents were brought together by the counselor to discuss the ambivalence and apparently mixed feelings that they held with regard to Sandy's getting a job. As it developed, the job symbolized for Sandy and her parents Sandy's move toward adulthood (the symbolic importance of a job can be very great). As this realization began to develop, Sandy was able to stop sending double messages to her parents (I am a child, no, I am an adult) and vice versa.
>
> In a short time following the resolution of the mixed feelings on this issue, Sandy found a suitable part-time

job. The fact that Sandy worked well, earning raises and minor promotions, did much toward helping her develop feelings of competence and confidence.

The inclination of parents to underrate their own teenager's maturity is understandable for another reason. Adolescents frequently behave more childlike toward their parents than toward other adults or peers. So parents are often not in a good position to see their own child's growth. They may even be envious of the apparently greater maturity they see in other people's teenagers.

Parents and their teenagers are like intermeshing gears. The drive shaft of the young person's gear begins to turn faster than the drive shafts of the older people, as the adolescent's rate of change accelerates. With gears, as with human beings, such a situation almost inevitably generates friction. And friction generates heat, which can cause a breakdown in the system. Counselors working with adolescents see many such breakdowns between parents and their adolescent children.

Understanding the process that your young person is going through can help you understand the sources of sullen, negative, and oppositional stances toward authority (reality). This in turn should help you to weather the emotional storms and to take your child's resentment or anger less personally. Even though a child seems to know instinctively exactly which buttons to push to upset a parent.

Psychotherapists are trained not to take the irrational resentments of their clients personally. To do so would undermine the therapeutic enterprise by creating defensiveness and resentment in the therapist, which would validate the client's feelings of anger, and so on, in vicious circle fashion.

It is to be hoped that your parent-child transactions include a rational discussion of any issue to be decided. But following this discussion comes the time when your parental decision has to be made. If the decision is counter to what your young person desires, so be it. You must be ready to hold firm

against the wave of pressure, ranging from sullen pouting to extreme verbal abuse, which tends to follow any decision that runs against the wants of the young.

Remember that it is not necessary, nor is it likely, that your adolescent will always agree with your decisions. But this is child-raising, not a popularity contest. Try to be calm and firm. Your attitude should be that a decision has been made, and barring new information which might alter that decision, that is that. Additionally, your word and deed must convey the attitude that negative, irrational behavior will not be rewarded, will not "win." Remember that you are serving, consciously or unconsciously, as an example for how one behaves under pressure.

If we parents "blow up" and yell, scream, and have tantrums, then how are our children to learn appropriate behavior? You do not meet anger with anger, or irrationality with irrationality, if you are to be useful to young people in guiding them toward more mature attitudes and behaviors.

CHAPTER 6

"Almost" (But Not Quite) Logic: The Slightly Separate Reality of the Teenager

---

"Contrariwise," continued Tweededlee, "If it was so, it might be; and if it were so, it would be; but as it isn't it ain't. That's Logic."
Lewis Carroll, Alice Through the Looking Glass

Reasoning with a child (or teenager) is fine, if you can reach the child's reason without destroying your own.
John Mason Brown

I think my parents ought to give me money and a car whether I work or not. After all, they have money and cars, don't they?
California teenager

The adolescent does not, as a general rule, think in quite the same manner as either a younger child or an adult. Considering all we have said so far about adolescence as a time of transition from childhood to adulthood, this statement may come as no surprise. In fact, you may already have come to this conclusion through dealing with your own teenager.

The scientific argument for adolescence as a time of *thought* transition begins with the work of such influential psychologists as Dr. Jean Piaget and Dr. Bruno Bettelheim, who studied the thought processes of children. They inform us of what you may regard as obvious, that children think differently than adults. If this is so, then there must be some

transition period during which the thought patterns of the child begin to evolve into adult-type thinking. The principal time for this major alteration in thinking about (and thus dealing with) one's internal and external environments is during adolescence.

Of course, we humans never reach a state of full "logicality." To do so, we would have to become computers. With the exception of *Star Trek's* Mr. Spock, few adults may be said to be really logical, rational creatures. At various times, in varying degrees, and in different circumstances, we all demonstrate traces of the illogical, narcissistic, and highly emotional thought patterns of childhood. Mr. Spock, of course, has the advantage over us Earthlings inasmuch as he is part Vulcan, a highly logical and emotion-free race of beings.

Possibly the idea that thought patterns undergo major changes during adolescence is a new consideration for you. However, it seems logical to assume that there is *some* time when the cognitive processes of childhood transform themselves into those of adulthood. Since we can see the adolescent's physical changes, as well as the tremendous emotional adjustments and readjustments being made during this period, it is also logical to assume that the young person's actual manner of thinking is undergoing a change as well. There is no more likely time, as I see it, for such a transition to be taking place.

The best argument for this can be seen in the interactions between teenagers and adults when they attempt to communicate in a rational and logical fashion. You are most likely to have such a conversation with your own teenager when there is a difference of opinion over something the teenager wants. It is often at these times, when your adolescent sincerely wishes to be logical and persuasive, that the "almost" type of reasoning is most apparent. While seeming to make some logical sense, or trying to, what comes out is a form of pseudologic that may puzzle or infuriate you. Your negative reaction may have a similarly negative effect on the teenager,

who has *satisfactorily* "explained" the particular situation and is stymied and frustrated by your apparent stupidity in not seeing the points so clearly made. Obviously, if one person in a conversation is using one form of logic and the other person is using another form, severe communication problems can be expected. You may be thrown off by the appearance of logic in what your young person is saying. You may also be puzzled by adult or almost-adult physical appearance. For example, at the time of this writing my 15-year-old son towers several inches over six feet tall and it is very easy to make the mistaken assumption that he is a grown man, an adult in all respects, including logical thought processes.

My son, however, exhibits adult-type logic only infrequently, though things are improving gradually as he grows older. Still, his view of the world and mine are so different that they constitute remarkably different perceptions of why and how things can and should take place in this universe. If I were to assume that my son and I were on the same logical wavelength, it would be a foolish assumption indeed. He uses a kind of "near" logic. He does not perceive or seem concerned about things that seem to matter to me. If he goes to an outdoor concert which is to be held at night, but leaves for the concert in the warmth of the afternoon, he often does not anticipate that it will grow chilly in the evening. Consequently, my suggestion that he take a sweater or coat, a suggestion offered in the mildest and most benevolent way, falls on deaf and sometimes even hostile ears, my concern sometimes being rewarded with a kind of modified snarl from my teenager.

However, I have concluded that there is some benefit in an adult's dealing rationally with a teenager, just as if the teenager too were using adult-type logic. Because even though the experience can be difficult emotionally for both parties, the teenager is nonetheless being exposed to an example of logical thinking. Over many years this rationality will be internalized, understood, and used. Of course, if the adult is emotional and irrational, the teenager will probably learn

little from the discussion except emotionality and vexation. It takes a rational and calm person to teach a younger person how to become rational and calm!

A humorous example of adolescent logic is seen in the following exchange between Vinnie Barbarino and Mrs. Kotter on the *Welcome Back, Kotter* television show:

"I moved out so my mom would have one less mouth to feed.
"She must miss you."
"No, I see her every night when I go home for dinner."

One of the reasons this strikes us so funny is that we recognize Vinnie's logic as being very close to real-life adolescent thinking. Even teenagers laugh at it, perhaps partly for the same reasons adults do, but still do not recognize pseudologic when they use it themselves.

My wife and I were visiting friends for dinner one evening when we overheard the following interaction between our hostess and her teen-age daughter:

"But, Mom, I have to go out tonight. It's a *must.*"
"You haven't done your homework. You've got to do the homework."
"I'm doing OK in everything except English, and that last grade wasn't my fault."
"Wasn't your fault?"
No. It was the teacher's fault. If she hadn't assigned that many pages, I'd have done OK."

I believe that such a statement is basically sincere, rather than basically devious or even stupid. It contains strong elements of the magical, wishful thinking of childhood. She wishes that reality were not reality. She wishes, *and somehow believes*, that it is the teacher who is at fault. Such magical thinking is often a major ingredient in adolescent pseudologic.

A parent who is not fully aware of the incomplete logic

system of his teenager may react with exasperation and other emotionality. When this happens a negative snowball is created which can gather its own force of angry words as it rolls along. As anger on both sides goes up, logic goes down. Positive and meaningful communication between parent and teenager is short-circuited, often turning into annoyance and bitterness. Unfortunately, such interactions tend to be fre quent between parents and their teenagers. And when the grownup becomes angry and irrational, all that is learned by the young person is that adults are usually rigid and unreasonable. This is just the opposite of what most of us are trying to teach our teenagers.

Illustrations of adolescent "almost" rationality abound. You could probably add many examples from your own experience. Here is another from mine.

When we returned from a two-week vacation, my wife and I discovered one of our teen-age sons had given a party in the house against our definitely expressed wishes. In discussing the incident, the boy professed not to be able to see anything amiss about his behavior and failed to understand why we were upset with him. Our words about "trust" and "mutual confidence" and so on were like talking into the wind. Our son's standpoint, as he expressed it was, "I deserve your trust now because I showed you that I could have a party and *nothing happened to the house."*

To this repeatedly expressed remark, I countered with the analogy of someone's borrowing a car without permission and without insurance, and the fact that he returned the car safely did not make the borrowing of it all right. Our son rejected the analogy, repeatedly stating, "Nothing happened, so the party was OK." Later he altered the situation by redefining 'party,' saying, "It was only a 'gathering.' A party is when you have a keg and a band and people come from all over. I only had 20 or 30 people, no band, and it was not a party."

We were at loggerheads. By our son's definition, he had had either a party or a gathering, both of which we had

expressly asked him not to have while we were away. Now what to do? Should we punish, and if so, in what way? How might we turn this into some kind of constructive learning experience for our son?

In this case, my wife and I stuck to our guns and defined the situation in terms of our adult logical standards, whether our son accepted such standards or not. We attempted to broaden the "lesson" by pointing out that in the world there were almost always consequences to one's behavior. Additionally, these consequences were frequently inflicted whether one felt they were fair or not, or even when one did not fully understand them. We told our son that we could not agree with his thinking in the matter. We pointed out that outside the family, behavior like his might lead to dire consequences, such as the loss of a job, the breakup of a relationship, or the loss of other people's trust.

Our son was angry that we, as he perceived it, would not see his point. We nevertheless felt that he learned more from our calm and reasoned response than he would have from an angry, punitive shouting match. For direct punishment, we did nothing at all. He was in his logic system, we were in ours. For the moment, our son had lost our trust. We had our statement to make and we made it. In years to come, our son's form of logic (illogic?) will change and this confrontation may have been useful.

There is no question that the pseudologic of an adolescent is frequently aggravating. But loss of control by the adult is not helpful. What is most useful, to you and your teenager, is immediately to identify in your own mind the as-if nature of the teen-age logic system. Quickly remind yourself that as teenagers they do not have full and complete logic systems. They are in a process of changeover from the thought patterns of childhood to those of adulthood. They need good guides or models for clear and logical thinking, rather than angry examples of adult temper tantrums. They may not, under the best of circumstances, come to see the point that you wish to make. Then, keeping all of this in mind, you

should: (1) try to stay calm and rational; (2) provide some negative consequences for the teenager's behavior if this appears warranted; (3) provide a model for dealing with the situation in a calm, logical manner, and (4) if possible, generalize the specific instance to the broader situation such as, in our son's case, the potential loss of trust by others outside the family.

In sports, the coach runs over the play patterns again and again in order for his players to learn to function smoothly in the game. The analogy holds true for thinking. Although you can't force your teenager to run through all the thought patterns of logic, you can be the coach who demonstrates rational patterns again and again. Gradually your young person will begin to grasp the nature and structure of logical thinking of the day-to-day variety. This means understanding the consequences of behavior, practicing planning and foresight, and gaining some ability at vicarious problem solving, in order not to have to learn everything the hard way through personal experience.

You should not take these suggestions as the only "correct" or "right" ways to handle your teenager. I do not know exactly what is correct or right. I know only that if my goal is to assist the development of young people from the dependent and often illogical state of childhood to the more independent and more rational state of adulthood, I must attempt to control my own emotions, think clearly, and provide as good an example as possible in often rather tense interpersonal situations.

Here is another example of as-if, magical thinking. A 16-year-old stated to his parents and his teachers that it did not matter if we went to school, learned, or studied, because he was "going to become an artist." Rational arguments about the necessity for basic training in the liberal arts, about developing a portfolio, and about working more consistently on more artistic techniques only changed the young man's tune to this statement: "I *am* an artist." At this point, he had confused the word with the deed. If he named himself an

artist, he was an artist. It mattered not that no one else in the world considered him an artist. Perhaps great geniuses get away with this kind of thinking and make it stick. Most of us, not being great geniuses, have to do the best we can with plain old day-to-day logic. Actions speak louder than words. In reality, the boy will become an artist by producing some art, not by saying that he is an artist.

I should quickly note that this type of thinking is not limited to adolescents. Many adults also confuse the word and the deed. If they *say* they are someone or have done something or are going to do something, the words often substitute for the deed. After all, it is easier to talk than to do. The point is that this is still pseudologic, although this kind of thinking is more prevalent among teenagers than among adults. Kind and reasonably logical adults can often help teenagers move past the point of such "almost" logic. When a youngster does not find his way past this point and continues to use pseudologic into adulthood, the tendency eventually can become too deeply ingrained to be altered. Many people go through their entire lives kidding themselves that their words equal actions. They kid themselves, but few others are fooled, and such thought patterns are often destructive for those who do not outgrow them.

It is sometimes interesting to speculate on the beginnings of aspects of human behavior. As I mentioned, the apparent shift from child thinking to adult thinking was noted in the works of the Swiss psychologist, Dr. Jean Piaget. For the most part, Piaget concerned himself with mental and moral development. He noted a shift in moral values at about age 12, supporting the notion that the source of the adolescent's value system gradually moves from parents to peers during the second decade of life.

Dr. Marshall McLuhan studied the effects of technology on culture, and he has written about some of the things that have an impact on the minds of our young people during childhood and adolescence. McLuhan theorized that the way information is presented has an effect on the way it is pro-

cessed by the mind. He explained that after the printing press was introduced and the printed word became the primary medium of information, the human mind exposed to print and to reading tended toward a more rational and linear processing of information. In other words, a person started at one point and read (and thought) his way to another point. In a book, information is presented in a serial, linear, connected form. Each word, sentence, paragraph, page, and chapter is followed by another, and they all lead progressively to some degree of coherent sense.

But, McLuhan pointed out, the advent of television gave us a nonlinear, nonrational, multisensory electronic bombardment of information, rather than the connected, progressive ideas presented in books. Further, the control of the *rate* of information impact and processing is taken out of the passive TV viewer's hands (or head). Unlike the reader who can control the flow of material, digest, rethink and reread it, the television viewer must go quickly with the material, absorbing its visual and auditory impacts instantaneously and with little chance to do more than form quick impressions of whatever is being presented.

McLuhan said, in effect, that the manner in which information is presented *influences the manner in which a person actually thinks*. In other words, a generation of television viewers might well *think* differently from an older generation brought up principally on books!

Let's say that the mid or late 1950s was approximately the time when, in this country, television began dramatically to supersede reading in the early lives of many of our children. If McLuhan is correct, then we might expect some evidence of a change in rational thought processes from that generation on.

Such evidence is difficult to present from a standpoint of "hard" data, that is data which would withstand the test of scientific scrutiny. Little such scrutiny is presently being carried out, to my knowledge. But sometimes "soft" data has its place too. Consider the fact that it is estimated that the young child spends some 3,000 to 4,000 hours viewing television,

for an estimated total of some 12,000 to 15,000 hours viewed before graduation from high school. Contrast these figures with the estimated 4,000 to 5,000 hours spent in school classrooms from kindergarten through high school, and it can be seen that TV might be a powerful and seductive force. TV may have more impact on our young children and teenagers than books, teachers, or parents!

There is a consistent trend toward lower reading scores among California high school students, as well as among students in other parts of the country. There is a continuing general decline nationwide in scores on the Scholastic Aptitude Test. Universities have to implement remedial reading and writing courses for many of their almost illiterate incoming freshman.

If television is not actually changing the thought processes of our children, certainly something is keeping them away from printed material. And to stay away from reading and writing while staying immersed in music, TV, and marijuana is dangerous to one's brainpower.

I do not want to indict television alone, for there seem to be other factors about our culture that contribute to the decline in basic reading and writing skills. They too may be shaping new attitudes and possibly generating markedly different conceptual patterns from those of most of us who grew up in an earlier time.

One major competitor for the time and attention of teenagers is rock music and its various offshoots, such as Punk and New Wave. This music is a competitor that may rival TV in its impact.

The music boom, with its proliferation of records, tapes, concerts, and expensive sound equipment, is a major activity and central force for many adolescents. It is very important to them.

But what is the nature of the music? What is the message?

We are not talking about genteel drawing room music, a Bach fugue, or a careful Mozart piece; nor are we talking about Sousa marches or Crosby ballads.

We are talking about music of a powerful, driving, anti-intellectual, typically antiestablishment, narcissistic, and pleasure-seeking kind. It is the music and lyrics of the dispossessed, the angry, and the self-indulgent. It also seems to be closely tied in with the use of marijuana and other drugs. It is the fashion to be "laid back" (a psychologist might call it withdrawn), while listening to records and smoking a joint. In general, TV, rock and marijuana appear to contribute heavily to the thought patterns, attitudes, and behaviors of the young of today.

Here I am attempting to sketch out some of the major and important variables which seem to impact our culture and the adolescents of our time. And I am trying to assess and understand this impact. Naturally, what any of these variables means in the life of any given person is highly individualized. One person may indulge in enormous amounts of TV watching in order to compensate for lack of a social life, effectively avoiding the important struggles of coping and learning. Another may need drugs such as marijuana, Valium, or Quaaludes to get through the stresses of the school day, and later come home to "kick back" with stereo headphones, shoving noise into the brain and shutting out thought—shutting out thinking. Another may have an allergic reaction to marijuana, technically a "toxic psychosis," and freak out badly.

To be sure, many young people handle their drugs, their TV, and their music and at the same time deal effectively with their school work and athletic endeavors. In my experience, these people are rare. They are often very superior people intellectually. Tragically, however, I have seen even many truly gifted young people dope themselves so heavily with drugs, TV, or rock music that they have seriously impaired their ability to think in a powerful, analytic fashion. Although these teenagers are not derelicts by any stretch of the imagination, they will never reach the potential they showed before they became involved in the laid-back world of nonthought and little effort.

These observations are based on my own experience with adolescents—my children, their friends, and the many young people with whom I have worked professionally over the years.

Perhaps I have underplayed the teen-age ability to read and write. Many adolescents read and write well and thoughtfully. However it is my strong impression that for the vast majority of teenagers, reading is not a really important factor in their lives, and generally plays a secondary role to television, music, drugs, and peers.

So I am suggesting that the modern adolescent may actually process information in a different manner from most of the current adult population. That is, the modern teenager *thinks* differently than people in older generations.

Influences such as TV, drugs, and rock music are all *interacting* in the young person during a turbulent time of psychological and physiological change. If there are hormonal changes and obvious body changes, why not brain changes, too? But if the brain changes, what sort of changes are taking place? Is the natural, normal, "spaciness" of teenagers related to some underlying neurological shifts? Let's take a look at some of the very interesting ideas of a psychologist named Julian Jaynes.

Dr. Jaynes' area of research is left- and right-hemisphere functions within the human brain. The left hemisphere harbors the speech and language areas and may be considered to be the seat of rational, linear thought. The right hemisphere, on the other hand, according to Jaynes and the psychoneurologists who have devoted much study to brain functions, tends to generate the intuitive, nonrational, more "creative" modes of thought.

Interesting, yes, but what has this to do with the adolescent in modern times?

Several lines of thought converge. Jaynes' ideas blend with Freud's notions about the child's mind as spontaneous, nonrational, and emotional—all right-hemisphere characteristics. Piaget discusses the shift from the thinking of the child

to the different type of thinking of the adult. So what we may be observing in adolescent thinking is the gradual shift from right-hemisphere, global nonanalytic brain function to essentially left-hemisphere rational, analytic brain function.

If this is so, even in part, it would help account for some aspects of the adolescent's "almost" or "nearly" logic. But there is, of course, the experience factor to be considered too. For a young person can't be too perceptive and logical about complex issues or situations requiring experience.

Whether the shift in logical thinking is actually neurological or whether it comes about through increased experience, or both, adolescence certainly is a time of "thinking changeover."

From a practical standpoint, when as a parent you are engaged in what seems like a "logical" conversation with your young person, the logic part of the conversation may or may not be real. Adolescent logic is erratic—a now-you-see-it, now-you-don't phenomenon. However, do not be discouraged, even if your youngster confidently insists on the correctness of the pseudological viewpoint. Just present your argument in a calm and rational fashion and remind yourself that such discussions are good practice for both of you. Eventually the thinking shift occurs and the young person begins to get the idea of cause and effect—the fact that behavior has consequences—and the advantages of looking ahead and using vicarious problem-solving techniques. Looking before leaping becomes a more meaningful and appealing concept.

One final speculation. Some developmental researchers believe that there are critical periods in the stages of human development. I believe that adolescence is one such stage. It seems to me that the complexity and many delicate balances of adolescence have not always been sufficiently appreciated. And it may well be that some of the situations and influences that impact the young person have an irreversible effect. We adults need to give much careful and considerate thought to what we are doing with our adolescents, both at home and at school, and why.

I have offered several suggestions for ways to assist your teenager over this "logical hump" of adolescence. Let me offer one more thought.

If you can entice your young person to read and write more, this can be very important. Of course parents and teachers often pressure young people to read, and such pressure is often met with little enthusiasm. Perhaps nothing can compete with TV, drugs, and rock. Maybe even sex takes a back seat (pun intended) to these powerful, pleasurable stimulants.

However, I have found that if I can somehow encourage a teenager to keep a written journal of thoughts and feelings, this exercise pays good dividends. There is improvement both in written expression and in thinking skills. There are also gains in thinking ability and understanding of self. With understanding of self and greater thinking power come increased ability to think about others and understand the world.

I have already noted that many adolescents do think, write, talk, paint, and generally express themselves forcefully and beautifully. Nonetheless, there are too many teens who stand intellectually mute and creatively sterile. I believe that anything that parents and teachers can do to reverse this trend by helping to move young people toward increased written, spoken, or other forms of rational self-expression will be helpful.

CHAPTER 7

Future Shock

The pace of American life in general, still steadily accelerating, . . . has its effect on us (today's teenagers) also. We are lost inside this fast-moving, technological world that is taking away our identities. Computers, cars, television, telephones, atomic energy and pollution are all parts of our lives. We live in the science-fiction world that previous generations only read about. However, the increasing technology of today seems to be working against us. Progress has ceased to be a positive word. People no longer run the world, machines do. Machines run our lives directly or indirectly; and this has the effect of dehumanizing us. Growing up in this atmosphere gives us a sense of helplessness, of not being able to change anything.

Tied in with technological advancements in transportation is our subsequent mobility. This also has the effect of dehumanizing us, tearing us apart from one another, from our fellow human beings. Since our society is based on movement, many families are not able to live in the same place for more than a few years. Commuting to work and school is also very common, especially in the suburbs. Because of the relative ease of mobility in social status and miles, few relationships are permanent. Only surface, temporary relationships are possible. This leaves us with a great feeling of loss. We have no home, no place to come back to.

California teenager whose writing skills have obviously
not been eroded by TV, drugs, or rock music.

This is the first age that's paid much attention to the future, which is a little ironic since we may not have one.   *Arthur C. Clarke*

The future is very much on the minds of many young people today. Some teenagers feel there is no real future for them. They say that nuclear war, the energy shortage, inflation, and a tight job market create a bleak picture. Other young people, especially those in middle-and late-adolescence, try hard to plan what career to pursue, what school to attend, and what training to acquire, so that they will be prepared for the future.

Just a few years ago it was generally assumed that there would be work for all who wanted jobs. An ever-expanding economy seemed to guarantee steaks on every barbecue and two cars in every garage. The presumption of this guarantee is now gone, as extinct as the 6 percent thirty-year home mortgage. Today's young people worry about not being able to afford a garage, not to mention the house and car that go with it.

Has the future always been so much on the minds of so many young people?

This is a difficult question to answer. There is no real data in this area. However, it can be stated that many of the older generation have difficulty recalling that they worried much about what they would do or be when they grew up. It was assumed that knowledge of a trade, membership in a union, or a college degree would all be useful. This assumption too is now seriously challenged by today's tight job market.

At this juncture I must make a slight, but very serious, digression to note that we are talking here about the fortunate young people who do in fact still seem to have real options regarding their education or their careers. There are, however, a large number of young people whose choices seem at this time so limited and bleak that they may find it ridiculous to consider the future in terms of "career."

I am talking, of course, about poor people. The children of the poor tend to grow up aware of the sharp dichotomy between affluence and their own poverty, as well as of their apparent lack of opportunity within our system. For many of these young people, simple survival has a much higher prior-

ity than worrying about their future. We of the middle class may anguish about the cost of child rearing—buying clothes and food and summer camps and the like—but the poor anguish about life itself.

One can only empathize with the hurt and despair of poor parents, who not only feel that they have little to offer their children materially but who also perceive that the future of their children is likely to be grim.

Admittedly, it is hard to communicate hope when one has no hope. It is hard to feel up when one is down. It is hard to be a "good parent" when one is worn-out, harried and exhausted from the work of daily survival. Nonetheless, good parents come in all shapes and sizes and at all income levels. We all know the many stories of poor children nurtured on the dreams and hopes of their parents who managed to struggle and reach great heights. In any case, however one looks at it, poor children have greater burdens and fewer options than children who are economically secure.

But both rich and poor children today find themselves in a world they never made (which is true for all generations, of course), as well as in a world no other generation of young people has ever faced! I do not believe that there has ever been a generation of young people so beset by uncertainties and by the contradictions and tensions of affluence and poverty, education and ignorance, work and play. And there certainly has never been a generation so saturated at young ages by TV, music and drugs.

Where do we turn to get a handle on the situation? Are there any helpful ideas? How can we come to understand the situation our young people find themselves in? Can we help?

The situation has been growing on us for some time. In the 1970s, Alvin Toffler's book *Future Shock* helped many of us to understand better some of the sources of the stressed, tense, vaguely anxious feelings that we saw in others and often felt in ourselves.

Toffler says that in modern times the *rate* of life changes has accelerated beyond that ever experienced before. We live in a world of overstimulation, information overload and

transience. People move from one part of town to another, from one part of the country to another. People divorce and then remarry, spawning several sets of offspring, creating ever-widening circles of semirelatives. Too many decisions and an abundance of freedom give us the problem of over-choice. Old values fade and are replaced by new ones—or are not really, replaced at all. New life-styles arise. And so on. For Toffler, these situations are both symptoms and causes of a society suffering from future shock. In short, things and people change in our lives so rapidly that we have difficulty settling in and developing more or less fixed standards and routinized patterns.

Toffler also cites ongoing changes in "the hidden rhythm in human affairs that until now has served as one of the key stabilizing forces in society; the family cycle." He says that children growing up in a family once had a sense of continuity, a sense of what was expected of them, what their place was and would later be in relation to their own particular family. But with the general mobility of people and the changing nature of the family itself, we are no longer provided with this sense of knowing who we are and where we are going.

Not all of what Toffler wrote about is as obvious to us now as it was then, in the late 1960s and early 1970s. Outwardly, things have calmed down a bit. The cultural pendulum has been swinging in a more conservative direction, and some of the "old values" once again flourish in parts of our society. Nevertheless, change is here. We cannot un-invent television, un-explore space, forget the Beatles, ignore the impact of microcomputers, disregard miracle medicine, erase knowledge. For better or worse, our world still rushes ahead. For some of us, our own values may be hard to define and feel at ease with, when the cultural pendulum is swinging against change, for the dichotomies between opposite sets of values can pull us in both directions at once.

The high rate of social and technological change is especially hard on many adults who grew up enjoying slower and perhaps more comfortable ways of living. Our children

are much less aware than we are of the contrast between "the good old days" and today. It is interesting to speculate that, since our children were born into this phenomenon of rapid change and have known no other way of life, perhaps they are better adapted to it than we of the older generation. And perhaps to some extent it is *our* uncertainty that adds to *their* problems in dealing with today and tomorrow. Not only are we unsettled ourselves, we often cannot furnish our children with guidelines that are valid and meaningful in this new society. While, as individuals, young people are uncertain about whether they will be able to get jobs, function well, attain the standards of their parents, and so on, parents and schools are often guilty of actually aggravating the problems. We talk about the hard times to come in the world, how tough it is to make a living, that only those who do well in school and go to college can hope for real success, how high the cost of living is, how hard it is to make a buck. These "fright" comments are often intended to heighten anxiety in adolescents in order to motivate them into becoming serious about their preparation for the future. This usually means we want them to do well educationally, begin to plan for careers, and "get serious" about life.

It is obvious that every young person must eventually begin to set priorities and do some planning for later life. However, I question seriously whether early or middle adolescence is a necessary or even appropriate time for too much of this type of thinking. We would do well to consider the pressures we are putting on our young people when we indicate that if they haven't chosen a college or a career by 10th grade all is lost. Are such pressures really necessary? Some of these pressures only seem to add to the adolescents' problems of identity formation, dependence-independence conflicts, and their abundance of general anxieties.

It does not look as if the world stress level is going to decline in the near future. So I believe it would be more useful for us to develop some forms of "stress shelters."

We could all use some protected oasis to which we could

retreat from the stress of daily life. Undoubtedly each of us could think of several excellent ways to do this for ourselves. But, unfortunately, we probably cannot make such plans for our young people. This is because what is a stress shelter for one person is not necessarily a stress shelter for someone else. For example, sending a group of teenagers off for a few days of back-packing in the mountains might be relaxing for some but quite anxiety-producing for others.

Although it is difficult to say what a stress shelter might be for any other person, we as parents might do well to introduce the concept of *stress* to our children and teenagers. We humans tend to work better when we have labeled something. If we can get a word on it, we are half way to handling it. So, if a young person knows there is something out there called "stress," that individual is probably in a better position to deal with stress factors.

There is no help for it and no going back. Stress is in our lives and in all lives for the foreseeable future, an active, powerful, changing force. Of course, stress is not all negative, and some researchers feel that without a certain amount of stress our lives would not be as full and rich. I think that this is true. Yet it seems to me that many young people feel particularly *distressed* by the pressures of today's world. We should try to bring our teenagers to a conscious awareness that they can and must learn to deal with pressure in positive and productive ways. They need to learn that it is not necessary or helpful to "pot out" (use drugs) under stress, that stress is another problem that can be faced and resolved.

Adolescence is unquestionably a very highly stressed time of life. Because of the important identity transformations that take place during this period, the early- and middle-adolescent phases of development may be very poor times in which to pressure our teenagers toward long-range planning. Too many developmental factors are still operating and have not yet settled down. It would probably be much more helpful to most of our teenagers if we, as parents, would take a stance of benign tolerance toward adolescent confusions and uncer-

tainties about "life goals." Not knowing what one wants to do with one's life is not a crime. It is perfectly natural during the adolescent phase and even later on in young adulthood.

But our tolerance in this area should, as always, be coupled with a strong dose of expressed belief that ultimately the young person will "get the act together" and move toward productive and competent handling of various life choices.

This long-range *belief* in young people is vitally important. Yet it appears to be ignored or unexpressed by many parents. Some parents do even worse. They actively undermine the unformed and often shaky self-concept of their young people by implicitly or explicitly telling them what failures they are and expressing doubt and even contempt for their past, present and future.

> Fifteen-year-old Raymond had a father who more or less constantly remarked that the boy was a "loser." According to the father, he made these statements in order to help motivate his son toward performing better at school, smoking less marijuana and becoming more active socially. Unfortunately for the father and son, these statements had just the opposite effect on Raymond's developing self-concept. Finally, the young man became so enraged and resentful that he had to face a choice of either acting out his angry feeling on his father directly, running away from home, or "acting in" the hurt and resentful feelings on himself. For some time he did the latter. He increased his use of drugs, especially marijuana, and withdrew more and more into long periods of listening to music with headphones on while smoking joint after joint. He perceived this as the only viable solution to being goaded and emotionally bullied with the "loser" label. It was at this juncture that Raymond's parents requested counseling assistance.
>
> Through talks with his counselor, Raymond came to see why he behaved in certain ways. He began to understand that the primary stimulus for this behavior was his negative relationship with his father. Initially, Raymond tended to blame his father for all that was wrong in his (Raymond's) life. Gradually, Raymond came to

see that the ultimate responsibility for salvaging the pieces of his life and making something of them was his. A major part of the therapeutic work involved countering the father's negative influence on the boy's sense of self and assisting him to assess more objectively his own assets and liabilities. Raymond began to understand he was not a "loser" simply because someone else, even so important a figure in his life as his father, said he was. The self-fulfilling prophecy of "becoming a loser" could then be intercepted and reversed.

One of the most important and also one of the most difficult tasks in raising children is helping them find meaning in life. Those of us living and working with adolescents must take care in our attitudes and in what we say about the young person's current and potential competence for dealing with the complex tangle called "the world." What we say and do is often much more influential than we realize.

When Jerry was 13, his feelings about himself were definitely affected by one particular remark his father made. Jerry and his mother had been arguing over the purchase of scuba diving equipment; his mother argued against the purchase because of fear for her son's safety. The boy's father broke into the discussion with the memorable statement, "Jerry doesn't have to worry about drowning, he was born to be hanged."

Jerry, now an adult, states: "On the surface, this might definitely appear to have been an undermining statement. But on the contrary, delivered in that context and with my father's attitude of respect and confidence in me, I took that statement as supportive, a vote of confidence, a rather hell-for-leather type statement about who and what my father thought I was."

Another young man, Walt, was deeply affected by his father's oft-repeated statement, "If Walt can't do it, nobody can."

In each instance, the young man sensed that this was not just an empty verbalization on his father's part but rather a

deeply held attitude. This attitude expressed the feeling that the son could indeed handle the events of the world, including events of the future.

Since very little is constant in our world except change of one kind or another, should we not try to help our young people develop an *internalized constant,* an inner belief in their own ability to cope with the events and situations they will meet in their lives? It seems to me that this, not wealth or power, is the principal legacy that we adults can hand down to the younger generation. This internalized constant, this inner belief in oneself, is initially developed by parental confidence in the young person.

You as a parent must communicate this confidence to your teenager on a tolerant and long-range basis, expressing the feeling that he or she will, in fact, lead a useful and productive life and will ultimately take a place as a peer among adults. You must take the time to discuss things and, when appropriate, help with the initial steps. Elsewhere I have said that in good parenting, "less is more." But there are times when good parenting can involve helping your youngster move through some aspects of the world not yet experienced. School matters should be left to the teenager, since high school students have experience with schools of one sort or another for a period of nine to twelve years—that's a good deal of experience.

On the other hand, you might do well to participate, just as one would accompany any novice, in a first sailing excursion into the ocean, in an intial back-packing trip, or in that even more dangerous experience—a visit to a used-car lot. Your willingness to become involved can provide some very positive intergenerational contact. This in itself helps promote good feelings.

When you do these things, try to resist the impulse to suggest or correct. These are learning experiences, not final performances.

We adults are usually very concerned about preparing our children for later life. Generally, this means seeing that they

get good grades, perhaps go on to college, and ultimately find satisfying and financially rewarding careers. However, for the most part, such ideas seem remote and vague to adolescents, perhaps even disquieting and disturbing. To them "future" is a dark forest, a place in which to be tested and perhaps found wanting. The future is a place where they will have only minimal support from parents who have protected and supported them through the early part of life.

It is natural and understandable that they should want to put off or avoid too much serious consideration of the anxiety-provoking future and focus on the more immediate gratifications of the present, such things as music, sex, sun, surfing, skiing, partying, or what-have-you.

This adolescent tendency to want to spend time having fun is something we all share to some extent. Infants and small children, in particular, have a high drive toward immediate gratification. They want what they want when they want it. Adolescents, too, have difficulty putting off what they want. But I believe there is more to a teenager's impulsiveness and fun-seeking than simply a childhood trait not yet outgrown. It seems likely that the adolescent's difficulty in delaying gratification is also a psychological defense mechanism, which helps avoid anxieties associated with the problems of the "future."

Regarding the tendency of teenagers to do what they want when they want to, there is nothing parents really need to do. Teenagers simply mature out of those behaviors, given any reasonable reality-testing in their lives.

However, parents can help with the other cause of impulsiveness, which is insecurity about what the future may hold. They can help youngsters develop feelings of competence in their ability to deal with the complexities of the world, to handle relationships in positive and productive ways, and to function in a reasonably integrated manner intellectually and emotionally. From competence, comes confidence.

To achieve all this, young persons need to have frequent, consistent, positive contact with one or more adults, espe-

cially parents. These adults themselves must accept and understand the deep insecurities that are a part of life (not just the young person's life). If you are to be this helpful adult, you yourself must not be overwhelmed by anxiety. You must be willing to offer your teenager some assistance in coming to terms with life's ups and downs and especially with its uncertainties. You must also demonstrate your fundamental belief that these complexities, disparities, and mysteries can be integrated successfully.

CHAPTER 8

The Generation Gap

The only way to treat these little teen-age brats is to kick the holy crap out of them if they look at you cross-eyed.
A member of a California Police Department

"I just shoot the crap out of anyone who gives me a bad time."

"Yes, that is one way of reacting to a situation. But might there not be some other way?"

"Ain't no other way, Screw, 'em."

"But, if you try, you might come up with *some* other way, mightn't you? I ask this because human beings, as prone to violence as we may be, still have intelligence and can still *think* about various ways of behaving."

"Mister, you sure talk funny."

"Perhaps, but at least I *talk* first, not shoot first."

"Are you messing with me [dropping a hand over the six-shooter hanging off his hip]?"

"I wouldn't 'mess' with you. However, I would talk with you and reason with you. Any animal can fight and kill. Perhaps humans manifest such behavior with greater skill than most. However, the human animal can also talk and think and try to understand the words and the thoughts of other human animals."

"Sounds weird to me."

"Maybe. Maybe it is. But what makes us different from other animals, do you suppose?"

"Well I dunno. Mebbe talking and thinking."

"Mebbe."

An imagined dialogue between Socrates and Billy the Kid

Let's assume that for all parents a major goal in raising children is to assist them in developing the capacity to meet and creatively grapple with a changing world. Let's also assume that for the most part this ability is actually fostered through their contact with us—through what and how they learn from adults. We must then seriously consider the problem of the lack of intergenerational contact between the young and the old of our society—the problem of the generation gap.

Generally speaking, our society tends to be highly age-stratified. Our "senior citizens" are an especially visible case of such stratification. But our young children too are a separate segment of society, as are our adolescents. Of course, adolescents often seem to move themselves into a sort of self-imposed social exile, though how welcome most of them would be in adult company for any extended period of time is a moot point.

There are societies in which the young, old, and middle-aged are more mingled. It seems very likely that our own society in its beginnings in this country offered much more extensive, open and independent contact between generations. There was once a time when all able bodies were needed and a strong adolescent or two might make a difference in terms of whether a family survived or perished.

When people of all ages, especially the young and the strong, are needed in a society, there tends to be positive and meaningful contact between the generations. Also the young people hold a generally optimistic outlook about their place in that kind of society or, more broadly speaking, their ability to make their mark in the world.

Times have obviously changed. Currently we do not need adolescents as part of the work force on farms, in factories, and elsewhere, except in low-paying minimum-wage and/or

part-time jobs. Even the traditional valuation of the young as the warriors of a society has shifted. Technological advances in our weaponry systems has tended to diminish the need for youthful strength and raw courage, while putting a somewhat greater premium on advanced training, more education, and greater emotional maturity. One exception is in the case of fighter plane pilots, whose quick reflexes, youthful enthusiasm, and high aggressiveness make them militarily useful. Another exception which comes to mind is the recent Viet Nam War fought so bravely by so many young people, often those from the more disadvantaged sector of our society. Yet, the aftermath of this war did not see the young men who fought it glorified as warriors. Rather they tended to be degraded for their actions—perhaps a case of our own collective guilt and/or dissatisfaction with the war's course and outcome.

The fact is that may young people simply cannot find a place to work in our economy at the present time. Since a major part of the meaning of life lies in what we spend our time doing, usually work, what we *do* becomes largely who we *are*. This means that many of our adolescents may be at a serious disadvantage in developing feelings of identity and self-worth because our society hasn't much for them to "do" in the employment sense. They are not yet skilled in doing anything that society needs. Perhaps it is no wonder that the incidence of drug involvement, criminal acts, and emotional dysfunction, including a high suicide rate, is so prevalent among our young people.

> I can't get a job because I don't have experience. I don't have experience because I can't get a job. People ask me what have I "done." What can I say? I "done" been in school up to now? I "done" been a kid going with my parents to Disneyland and Magic Mountain up to now? I ain't "done" a murder, a robbery, or even a GTA (Grand Theft Auto). In some ways, I've done a lot of things. But, by some folks, I've done almost nothing, I guess.
>
> *16-year-old male*

The adolescent has not yet had time to accumulate a large achievement base, and since society has little use for unskilled services, is generally not given much of an opportunity to do anything except attend school. Thus, school achievement—whether academic, social or athletic—becomes the coin for evaluation of a young person's worth, particularly for self-evaluation. Without school success basic adequacy is questioned and self-doubts emerge. Confidence usually grows out of competence. And a person who has limited usefulness and limited ways of proving competence may well fail to develop a deep, internalized feeling of self-confidence.

Many adolescents feel acutely their general devaluation. This seems to be why so many young people have to "prove" themselves in various ways.

> I would shiv [knife] a dude who shows me no respect. No motherjumper can come on to my candy [girl friend]. Any sucker who does, dies.
> *17-year-old male in Los Angeles*

Because our society is so age-stratified, teenagers tend to be deprived of the kind of positive, meaningful, lasting, and deep relationships with older generations (including their parents) that might help them in their growing up. It's not, of course, that there is *no* contact between generations. But the contact can often appear to be somewhat arbitrary, authoritarian, or even directly negative, as when there is conflict with the police.

The adolescent's most frequent and consistent intergenerational contact is usually with parents. But parent-adolescent relationships are extremely complex bits of business, generally involving all sorts of surplus connotations, confusing emotional currents, and differing values and expectations on the part of all concerned. The final task of growing up involves the young person's emotional and economic break from parents. This is often a most difficult task, beset by mixed feelings. Because of these many complications between

parent and child, additional contact between the teenager and an objective, benign, wise adult "outsider" can be very useful. The general scarcity of such meaningful relationships is a serious lack.

What about our schools? These are places where teenagers and their instructors have a great deal of contact. Unfortunately, public schools, at least in large cities, seem to have become sterile, bureaucratic, rigid, and depersonalized institutions. The proverbial visitor from outer space might find many similarities between our prisons and some of our schools. This comparison is admittedly farfetched and not meant literally. But it is a fact that California law *compels* youngsters to attend school from age 6 to about age 18, offers virtually no due process procedures for redress of grievances between students and faculty, and permits the physical beating (the official euphemism is "spanking") of a younger person by an adult, although physical punishment of this sort is not officially allowed in either the penal or military systems.

Just writing these words causes me to be, once more, amazed at the manner in which our society "trains" its young. Is it any wonder that we have so much violence in our society, so little respect for knowledge and learning, so little attention given to the development of civilized and gentle treatment of one another?

The manner in which a society rears its young deeply reflects the values of that society. And those child-raising practices tend to perpetuate the society's values as well. In the home, part of current child-rearing involves a great deal of exposure to television. There is evidence that violence observed within families, on TV screens, and on athletic fields, breeds more violence. Also, as our society has become more impersonal, there is an increased tendency toward alienation.

Adolescence is already a time of high alienation. The teenager often feels euphoric at one moment, depressed at another. In some ways, the young person is at the mercy of

hormonal surges, often feeling estranged, rejected, and generally "weirded out." If parents can be helpful in only a limited way, or sometimes not helpful at all, we must look for help elsewhere. School is the primary institution dealing with our children. And even though schools do not seem to have a handle on what makes teenagers tick, some solutions for positive intergenerational contact may still lie there.

I believe that we should rethink our major educational assumptions in the light of our present knowledge about adolescents. Is a large and impersonal school the best environment for an alienated, unstable, rebellious, peer-oriented individual? It seems to me we could make a case for using the smaller, more intimate elementary schools for educating our teenagers, while turning the larger high schools over to the younger children.

The benefits for the teenagers might be considerable. Most notably, they would gain increased intimacy with adults who are not their parents. And these teachers, dealing with smaller numbers in a smaller environment, might be able to offer more compassion and more individualized instruction. They might deviate from a preset curriculum when necessary, stop to talk out a communication problem, and generally serve as models for how to handle oneself and other people.

We might then have fewer circumstances such as the following, as noted by one teenager:

> It's "Mr." this and "Mrs." that at this frigged off school. They load you up with busy work but they don't know you or care who you are as a person. Well, I care. I study them. I watch how they walk and talk. It's as if grown-ups get some sort of broomstick shoved up their ass. When they walk and move uptight enough, then they are pronounced "grown-ups." I'm telling you, man, just look at them. Watch those teachers move. Like they're robots. It's Sci-Fi time. Why don't they come off it? What are they afraid of? That the kids will do something to them? Hell, we aren't the enemy, but it often seems like we are fighting a war [with the adults].
> *17-year-old honors student*

A young child in elementary school needs individualized academic instruction in basic reading, writing, and math skills. But the teenager is often in desperate need of *individualized life instruction.* The teenager needs adults around who can impart a perspective on life (don't we all need such people?), someone who is a model for dealing constructively with the stresses of our current life and times, even someone who is willing just to spend some time "shooting the bull."

Ideally, of course, such a person would be the parent, but other people are needed as well. Teachers or coaches, have the potential for being powerful role models for young people. It is unfortunate that more adults, especially the "successful" ones in business, trades, sports, or the professions, cannot seem to find more time for meaningful interaction with young people. A discussion about drugs by a National Football League star in a sixty-second TV spot is not, I think, really a full exploration of the meaning, use, and abuse of drugs. But these adults are not at fault either, since our society provides no real bridge between young and old. Where, for instance, should a parent go to "hang out" more with the kids? The local park? You'd better not, for you'd probably be suspected of being a "narc" (Narcotics Agent) or arrested as a Dirty Old Man (or Woman).

Smaller, more intimate, and warmer school environments might go a long way toward helping steady some of the general turbulence of adolescence. The smaller school might also provide good adult-adolescent contact (on a first name basis), mild but immediate reality confrontations, and a general atmosphere more conducive to academic and social learning. In such a setting the adults might become oriented to young people rather than goal and grade oriented.

That is not to say that there are not many teachers and coaches, as well as others, who make meaningful contact with teenagers in large school environments. It is merely to note that a smaller, more intimate, perhaps more relaxed and casual environment might be quite useful in adult-adolescent interaction, with the primary goal being the development of

the young person as a whole person rather than as a halfback, or a scholar, or just one more face to talk to and one more paper to grade.

Doubtless there are many other worthwhile suggestions that could be made for fostering positive contact between teenagers and adults. One that seems potentially useful and which is being used extensively in West Germany even now is the work apprentice system. In such a system, the older worker teaches skills to the apprentice, obviously, but there is usually more to it than this. To teach almost anything on a one-to-one basis you have to relate pretty closely to the one you are teaching. When you relate closely to another human being, prejudices tend to go down and liking tends to go up. It seems to me that our society is heading toward a mildly anti-youth attitude. I think this is partly because we don't know our young people very well and, even worse, because we tend to be frightened by them. We adults are put off by the music and the manners of the young. They "do" drugs (while we have our beer or cocktails); they listen to loud and awful music (while we listen to old favorites of ours which *our* parents no doubt found "loud and awful"); and they watch too much TV and don't read enough (and we listened to too much radio or watched too much TV ourselves, and who read anything beside comic books unless your mother made you?).

Actually, the best person to whom a young person could "apprenticed" might be a parent. Most of us have a lot to teach our young people—everything from how to buy a used car (and not get taken) to how to fry a fish. It's just that things often get so *sticky* between ourselves and our teenagers. They seem to have so much to prove, so much over which to act defensively. We seem never to be able to say it right. There almost always is an edginess between parents and young people, the crust of the "edge" often breaking into an argument. And later we say to our spouse such things as, "I didn't *mean* for it to end that way, I was only trying to point out how to do it right." And the

youngster is off somewhere, feeling hurt and misunderstood, saying to some friend, "My old man [or old lady] is just too much. Always critical. I can't do anything right."

Such interactions between parents and teenagers go on all the time. Parents might, just might, do somewhat better if they understood the adolescent phase better. However, such understanding is absolutely no guarantee of any great degree of success at communicating with your young. Rather, it may, at the very least, keep you from having hurt feelings and, even better, keep you from saying or doing anything that pushes matters too far and further reduces the chances of any meaningful communication with your teenager.

The following is an example of a kind of nice, benign, and calm form of the parent teaching relationship I have in mind. I overheard this father-son interaction at a boat ramp. "Dad, why does it matter if all those ropes and lines are put a certain way on the boat? Why do you take so much time with them? Why not just toss them on deck?"

"Well, bub, you have to take care of things just in case you ever need them someday to take care of you."

Despite this rather graceful example of a parent interacting in a meaningful and positive way with a teenager, a generation gap does exist. This gap seems to involve in one way or another a variety of important topics: *work, sex, reality,* and *drugs.* These major issues are examined in the succeeding chapters.

CHAPTER 9

Work and Wealth

If one defines the term "dropout" to mean a person who has given up serious effort to meet his responsibilities, then every business office, government agency, golf club and university faculty would yield its quota.

John Gardner

I have always wished my parents had been rich, then I would not have had to work.

Jon Gardner

No other technique for the conduct of life attaches the individual so firmly to reality as laying emphasis on work; for his work at least gives him a secure place in a portion of reality, in the human community.

Sigmund Freud

For most of the world, to live in a nice home in a nice (non-violent) neighborhood, to live in a room of one's own, to have the use of a car, to have access to a sophisticated stereo system and a color television set, to take vacations, to have one's hair styled, and to wear stylish clothes, is to be "rich." A large portion of our young people are rich from the standpoint of sheer material possessions.

Within such a home there may also be positive family interaction, negative family interaction, or something in between. However, what I am concerned with in this chapter is the effect of sheer material wealth on the attitudes of the young.

In many instances, young people (especially young males) appear to be overwhelmed by their parents' accumulation of wealth. Owning things often means social clout, and many parents are showing their children how much they value such clout and telling them that that's what life is all about. But whether one agrees or disagrees with a materialistic value system is beside the point here. The point is that many young people are intimidated by the fact that their parents, the father in particular, could and did acquire so many things.

Dr. Herbert Hendin, a specialist in adolescence, states:

> As far as adolescent males are concerned, I think it's becoming harder to grow up to be a man in this culture. The competitive pressures are great . . . an awful lot of middle-class kids don't think they can achieve middle class goals, certainly not to the traditional extent of a young man expecting to "go further" than his father. Competitive pressures may diminish the sense of masculinity and encourage a partial bowing out from the male role. Some men . . . insulate themselves from defeat by not pursuing career success.

Many young men have confided to me, sometimes tearfully, always fearfully, that they do not see how they can earn enough money to acquire that which their parents have acquired. One young man stated:

> I just look around the living room. How did my dad get enough money for the down payment on the house? How can I buy all those lamps, *lamps* for Christ's sake? Even toothpaste and toilet paper! Stuff! Stuff! No way I can do it. No way.

Parents, schools, and the adult community in general seem to send frightening messages to our young. From the schools, invariably the message is: without a good education you will fail; without a high school diploma you cannot even hope to start on the success ladder; a college degree is the minimum for success ("success" usually meaning earned income); a graduate degree is desirable; et cetera and et cetera.

For the most part, parents have bought the academic argument. More degrees equals more money, although, as we have said, in the past decade or so this argument has become increasingly shaky. The downslide in job opportunities and income in some professions, such as teaching for example, has been matched by an upward acceleration of income in the blue collar and trade areas. Another teenager states:

> My parents want college for me. They tell me pot has affected me. Lowered my motivation or brain power. I don't think it's so. I just don't like to read and I don't like to study. Bus drivers make over $20,000 per year now. What's wrong with bus driving? I really want to go into something to do with forestry. But my dad says it's no money. Go into law or accounting, he says. But I don't like school. I got bad grades. I just can't sit still and study. He says forestry won't earn me a decent living. But why not? Maybe I just don't want as much as he did.

We talked earlier about how we of the older generation too often attempt to impose a bit of fear conditioning on our children. Admittedly our motivations are good. We want to influence our young persons to follow paths that will "maximize potential." The message often emphasizes the struggles and hardships of life. We also convey the message that we want our young persons to choose mates and careers that make them happy. Our "be happy and productive" doctrine seems valid for the most part. It's just that we adults have a way of deciding for our children what will make them happy or productive. And if our children are not following our implicit track, we tend to worry that they are off the track.

Worse yet, we adults often steal *hope* from our young. We worry aloud and excessively about mortgages, the general rack and ruin of the world, and some combination of nuclear disaster, race riots, oil shortages, and world famine. It may be that we are setting the stage for self-fulfilling prophecies in these areas by draining our youth, the ultimate strength and

hope of our society, of their own hope for a good, strong, and positive future.

Dr. Bruno Bettelheim touches on the very core of our children's problems, as well as our own, in facing this uncertain world: "Only hope for the future can sustain us in the adversities we unavoidably encounter."

Among the problems that confront our young people in the external world, work, sex, and drugs loom the largest and most immediate. Issues arising in these areas must be faced and resolved in some way in order for the young person to grow up. Moreover, these external problems interact with the turbulent internal problems of adolescence.

What a teenager eventually does in life, in a society with many options and many pressures for material success, becomes a pressure in and of itself. Out of their own anxieties, insecurities, and personal or job-related disappointments, adults sometimes pressure their young people to make career decisions early. For example, most high schools and all colleges and universities insist on a youngster's commitment to a major field of study. If he or she is not planning to go on to college or university after high school, there are often rather strong pressures, usually from parents, to choose a trade, get some vocational training, and get a job that "goes somewhere."

Not that all of this is all wrong. The reality of today's world is that early planning and careful career organization often does pay off monetarily and emotionally. Nonetheless, we must recognize that forcing them to make decisions puts real pressure on our young people. It is pressure because it heightens anxiety about the future, lending sometimes dark overtones to skies that were bright and sunny. Again, we have the impingement of reality on the young person's awareness.

Even so, most adolescents tend to feel more comfortable if they have made some choice about what they are going to do when they finish school, whether high school or college. This is understandable when you account for the relation-

ship between our self-value and our work. There may be people—philosophers or individuals buttressed by religious frameworks—who have reached a point in their thinking where there are absolute values and where a person's self-worth is a given, not something to be earned. Such thinking and such value systems are not the norm in our society, however.

There are adolescents at the high school and college level who renounce external standards of achievement such as grades, money, athletic awards, or other prizes, and embrace some form of spiritual "higher order" of thinking and values. I do not see this as an actual spiritual quest. I see it rather as part of a vitally necessary psychological defense for some young persons. In a society that values achievement and accomplishment, if people have had little time to accomplish much, they may perceive themselves as being of little value compared to high achievers such as parents. Rejection of adult achievement goals and withdrawal into spiritualism is one way of handling this type of pressure.

We must take care not to overawe and pressure our children with our buying power. Remember that buying power is sometimes a symbol for virility. And a parent's income and competence (virility) can be castrating for those who have not yet achieved either a state of high income or a state of high competence. Some parents seem, perhaps unconsciously, to take pleasure in putting their teenagers in their place. When the parent says to the young person, "All this is yours," it can also be interpreted as saying "All this is yours *to use* and has been earned by my power."

It also seems an unnecessary burden to place career choices about the necks of our already struggling young. Most of us more or less blunder or back into our careers anyway. Dr. Seymour Sarason, a psychologist at Yale University, and his colleagues are now leading the way toward alternative ways of thinking about one's career. Sarason especially notes that the old idea of "one life, one career" no longer necessarily holds. Dr. Robert Coles, in his biography of the great

psychologist Dr. Eric Erikson, points out that Erikson went through a protracted period of what would today be called an adolescent identity crisis. He survived it without a nervous breakdown or the heavy use of drugs or attempted suicide, and went on to make major contributions in the field of psychoanalysis and psychology. It should also be noted that Erikson apparently received little parental pressure and much parental support (including support from his stepfather) during this trying period of his life.

We need to give our young people time to experiment in finding their way, to try out a little of this and a little of that. Parents must communicate to their teenagers in word and attitude that, for the most part, there is no great hurry to decide on what one will do or be. Matters of this sort will unfold gradually.

At the same time, we ought to encourage our young in perseverance, industry, intelligence, creative planning, reliability, and so on. These are old virtues but noble ones. As with the Boy Scout Oath, they are tried and true.

It is often useful to remind young people of the lack of real competition in the world of work. There are few people who seem able or willing to give an honest day's work for an honest day's pay. If my pool man just comes and cleans the swimming pool on time and in a proper manner, I find myself talking to friends about what a great pool man I have. In short, people who just do the job they contracted to do get praised, since such responsible behavior tends to be increasingly unusual in our world.

We parents need to offer our young some perspective with regard to inflation, buying power, the price of homes, and so on. A great many adults did not purchase a home during the first few years after graduation from high school or college. In fact, my hunch is that those who made such purchases were the exception, not the rule, and that most of them were assisted by loans from parents. It is helpful to point out that a great many people simply have to work and save and plan for five or even ten years after becoming adults (in the employ-

ment sense) before they are able to consider so major an investment as a home.

We would do well to help our young people begin to understand some of the complexities of the financial world, such as interest rates, checking accounts, and the dangers of easy credit. Part of constructive intergenerational contact is for the elders to prepare the youngsters for survival in whatever society they happen to live. In our society, it is highly adaptive for our young people to be provided with a great deal more exposure to: (1) knowledge of human behavior—why people (including themselves) do what they do and feel as they feel; and (2) knowledge of basic business practices.

I like my suggestion about more knowledge of human behavior much more than I like the one about basic business practices. But both suggestions are realistic, to the point, and helpful in terms of functioning well. A rounded-out feeling for the arts and literature and a knack for building things are useful too.

In a chapter on work and wealth we are implicitly talking about what the young person is going to *be* in the career sense. The need for immediacy, noted elsewhere in this book, tends to get in the way of career development with many young people. It seems to me that very few young people possess the concept that one starts at, or near, the bottom of some career and gradually works one's way to the top. To be a rock musician, for instance, requires natural talent and also the dedication necessary to nurture and develop that talent. It takes years of lessons, practice, and often working for nothing or next to nothing in the initial phases, just to gain experience.

In other words, I am saying that the old idea of a job or career being developed in slow, incremental steps seems to have been taken over by an instant gratification concept that declares: "If I want to be an artist (or a rock musician or whatever) then I am one, simply by giving myself that label." Everyone seems to want to *be* something, missing the point

that you have to *become* something or someone, usually after a long apprenticeship and much sacrifice and hard work.

For many people in our society "more is never enough." If we have trained our young toward a philosophy of "more," we have trained a group of malcontents. In considering how to counsel our young people about affluence, we might want to give careful thought to the ideas of Marshall Sahlins in *Stone Age Economics.* Sahlins defines affluence as a condition "in which all the people's material wants are easily satisfied." He points out that there are two ways to achieve this condition. One way is to produce much, and the other is to desire little. In the first way, we close the gap between what we have and what we want by producing more. The second way is the Zen road, in which our wants are few and we can "enjoy an unparalleled plenty—with a low standard of living."

The trick, of course, would be for us to develop a sense of satisfaction with a world of more modest external trappings and fewer technological toys. It seems difficult to move in this direction, what with the barrage of advertising and consumption pressure that surrounds us all. Nevertheless, the subject deserves much discussion between adults and young people.

CHAPTER 10

Sex

I hate to admit I was intimidated by a tight ass in tight pants. But I was intimidated by a tight ass in tight pants.
18-year-old male in Beverly Hills

Most of the guys just want to jump your bones. They don't know beans about relationships, about a little *caring*. The ones who seem to have gotten it together enough to know about tenderness are too old; the ones who still turn me on are too dense and insensitive to believe.
16-year-old girl in Malibu

Oh, she doth teach the torches to burn bright!
It seems she hangs upon the cheek of night
Like a rich jewel in an Ethiop's ear;
Beauty too rich for use, for earth too dear! . . .
Did my heart love till now? Forswear it, sight!
For I ne'er saw true beauty till this night.
Romeo, 14-year-old in Verona, Italy

The exquisite sweet-sour pains and joys of adolescent sexuality can be recalled with wry pleasure by most adults. These feelings continue to be sources of instruction and delight in various beautifully etched plays, books, and films such as *Romeo and Juliet*, *Going All the Way*, and *Summer of '42*. The intense, bittersweet, usually confusing and frustrating emotions of awakening sexuality are obviously new to each young person experiencing them for the first time. These feelings, and their later elaboration into deeper

and more mature love relationships, constitute another major aspect of the cultural, biological, and personal rites of passage into which each young person must plunge at puberty and through which each must somehow find the way while growing up.

Most secondary schools offer great amounts of technical detail about how our bodies function sexually. Also,young people are exposed to high amounts of sexual stimulation in books and on the screen. Yet there still exists a great amount of misinformation and general ignorance on the part of young people about sex, as well as about intimacy and love.

So much has been written about the technical aspects of sexuality that none of it seems to need repeating here. And the happy publication of Eleanor Hamilton's book, *Sex, With Love*, finally gives us some excellent resource material for amplifying and underlining the many facets of sex, intimacy, and love.

It is unfortunately true, however, that our young people are seldom able to learn about love through observing it. Our cultural values still tend to regard as taboo the explicit depiction of lovemaking on TV or in the movies, though acts of literally awful physical mayhem may be acted out upon one body or another in almost endless amounts and with fine attention to gory detail.

By now this point has been made so many times by so many social commentators that it seems redundant to write about it at all. Yet anyone who works closely with young people in any capacity has to be shocked by television's tremendous impact on attitudes and behaviors. Book learning does poorly in competition with film or TV learning. Movies and TV are just too immediate, too graphic, and too easily available.

Let me quickly note that many movies and TV programs are very positive in the lives of our young people. I think it is likely that TV will ultimately replace books as the major means of transmitting technical information to the young of our culture, and this is not necessarily bad. Programs such as

The Waltons, Little House on the Prairie, Roots, and many others have contributed to the better understanding of ourselves and our heritage. Nonetheless, judging from much of the current programming, one might suppose that we were training our young for macho roles or to be sex symbols and how to deal with problems that can and must be resolved within a half-hour or hour time slot. In general, movies and TV do not really appear to offer teenagers direct and honest depictions of loving and lovemaking.

However, our new and more open approach to sexuality, including some of its raunchier aspects (portrayed with great humor in the movie *Animal House*), is movement in the direction of helping all of us better perceive loving sex as both natural and *fun.* As usual, there is trouble in paradise. Despite the so-called new sexuality, there are indicators that this may not be such an unmitigated blessing.

The idea that sex is a free and natural act, an extension of and a part of intimacy and love between two people, seems to me a gain over older attitudes that sex for pleasure and/or sex out of wedlock are sinful and wrong. Such ideas still exist but for the most part appear to be changing. For certain, they have greatly changed among the vast majority of today's teenagers. And however one feels about the moral aspects of sex, the plain fact is that a great many adolescents today engage in a great many sexual activities, including sexual intercourse. Such involvements are more common and start at an earlier age than when we of the older generation were teenagers.

The heightened sexual activity of the younger generation (and this is true of high activity levels in general) seems to be a facade behind which lie unresolved attitudes and more fundamental personal insecurities.

The negative fallout generated by open attitudes and early starts in sexuality appears to involve the boys as much as (if not more than) the girls. Early adolescent girls who become sexually active tend to handle the pressures and problems of

sexuality either by seeking more information from an older person (if such intergenerational contact is available) or more often by simply turning to an experienced and reasonably well-informed peer. The rise of the so-called Free Clinics and the Women's Rights movement has provided additional emotional support to young females as well as information about prophylaxis and hygiene.

On the other hand, young males seem generally less prone to seek intergenerational information or to avail themselves of professional consultation, either at Free Clinics or otherwise. Too often they seem to hold the attitude that in some strange and mysterious way, they are supposed to know all about how to do "it." Doubtless this is a holdover of the general burden of having to be strong, silent, and capable, which we have characteristically placed on males in our society. While fewer adults now consciously hold this position, role models for such "male" attitudes and behaviors still exist. These role models range from the idolization of professional athletes (especially professional football players encased in their modern armor and immersed in physical violence) to admiration for the deadly coldness and explosiveness of characters often portrayed by actors like Clint Eastwood—the cool, competent, never-at-a-loss, quintessential modern fighting man.

For most males of any age it is impossible to live up to such characters. In our vulnerability we identify with and admire their power. We wish deeply to have such power, including their ability with females. So in comparing himself with his ideal, and being inexperienced, the young man tends to be insecure. He is generally reluctant to seek advice and has no other resources for learning sexual and loving techniques. The young man tends to have his own ideas about what "super stud" role is expected from him by females. As you might guess, a very high-risk situation develops out of all this, hinging on the male's sexual performance or, worse yet, nonperformance.

In my professional practice, I have seen an increase in the past ten years from zero problems with adolescent male sexual dysfunction, excluding gender identity and homosexual difficulties, to approximately one of every three new cases involving an adolescent male. Such cases principally involve the typical old male bugaboos: premature ejaculation and/or failure to achieve erection.

In both instances, the youngster is often simply suffering from beginner's anxiety. Many young men feel that the women are experienced and that they expect a degree of sophistication in sexual technique that the young man knows he does not possess. Under such pressure, failure of erection or premature ejaculation is highly likely. As with males of any age, such "failure" often sets the stage for heightened anxiety under similar circumstances in the future. This anxiety then creates another performance failure. The performance failure lowers self-esteem and increases general anxiety and feelings of failure and stress. Ultimately, the cycle can lead to the young man's "solving" the problem by avoiding sexual situations, including social situations that might lead to an invitation for sexual contact. One 15-year-old, Don, a tall, handsome, shy young man stated:

> You can just be at a party, you know. Everything seems laid back. Mellow. Maybe you're dancing. Maybe just listening to the music. Then some chick maybe a little drunk, maybe doing Ludes [Quaaludes], hits on you. She might just say, "Want to get it on?" It happened to me that way the first time. We walked in a bedroom and she just got naked. Like that. That quick. I wasn't ready. I didn't know what to do. I took my clothes off. My mouth was dry. I wanted to go to the bathroom. I wanted to screw her. I didn't know what I wanted. I just know I didn't get hard. I was ashamed. She seemed sort of ticked off.

This young man began to avoid parties and any other social situations that might lead to a sexual invitation. He noted repeatedly (as have other young men of my acquaint-

ance) the sexual aggressiveness of young women. Since he is attractive, the girls seek him out. He finally adopted a "cool" attitude to indicate his lack of concern but which masked very deep worries about his sexual performance.

Counseling with most young men suffering from problems in sexual performance involves both instruction and support. The instruction deals with basic techniques and basic physiology, since it cannot be assumed that the youngster knows very much about either despite our growing cultural openness and the books available on the subject. Support is especially important from a warm, understanding older man who can empathize with the situation of the younger, less experienced one. One form of support especially useful to young men (and women) with whom I have worked on problems of sexuality is to contrast the 1950s approach to sexuality with that of the present day.

As an adolescent in the late 1940s and early 1950s, my sexual development and that of my peers was reasonably well protected and quite well structured. Like a careful fight manager who does not bring his fighter along too quickly by overmatching him against too much experience or too tough a foe, the rules of the times guarded us. The girls, for the main thing, were afraid of getting pregnant, their fear of this event being matched or even exceeded by that of the boys. The boys were generally haunted by the spectre of an outraged father tracking them down with horsewhip or shotgun in hand. But, beyond the ultimate mistake of pregnancy, one's sexual development could unfold in gradual, predictable, and often very pleasurable ways.

Everyone knew, for example, that no self-respecting girl would kiss on the first date. If a second and then a third date developed, then a good-night kiss or two would be in order. Note, also, the word "date." A date, as all older generations know, is a prearranged plan to go somewhere together at a prearranged time, usually implying involvement with the opposite sex. In the present decade, dating per se is, for the most part, in limbo. Most young people sort of just show up

at parties and mill around, usually drinking, smoking a little pot or "doing" some other drugs, dancing and talking, and just seeing what might develop.

For some teenagers, this kind of nonparty, nonplan works well. But for most, as far as I can observe, this does not work as well as the 1950ish dating situations.

For the uninitiated, it should be noted here in a brief digression that "party" and "to party" or "partying" have different connotations for the different generations. By those words, young people today generally mean to smoke marijuana together. Whether this takes place in a home, a car, at the beach or on a hilltop is all the same—it is "partying." Obviously, in 1950 a party meant something quite different, generally a group-gathering much more structured as to time, place, and dress.

It is interesting to note that the movie *Animal House* was a terrific hit with today's teenagers. Many teenagers who saw the film experimented with holding parties in the 1950ish sense, with the infamous toga party of *Animal House* offering a costume theme.

But to return to the analogy between the 1950 and the current structuring of sexual behavior—in the '50s a "nice" girl did not ordinarily "put out" (engage in petting behavior) unless she and her boy friend had dated a sufficient number of times to be considered to be "going steady." Going steady, of course, provided Saturday night security for both parties, as well as the equally important opportunity to begin to assess and explore the intricacies of a male-female relationship, including both the physical and the psychological complexities.

Informally, there were the "bases," which helped guide one's behavior and expectations to a large extent. For instance, a girl would not generally allow a boy to go to second base (feel her breasts) until they had been going steady for a month or two. The boy might expect to reach third base (manual exploration of the girl's genitals, including finger insertion) after having gone steady with her for three to

six months. "Home runs" were rare for the reasons already mentioned, and were often almost not worth it because of the anxiety one felt while waiting for a late period, wondering whether the rubber might have broken or leaked, or whether one had withdrawn in time. Oral sex was not particularly uncommon, nor was "making out" while completely nude. In these ways young people came to know gradually, through somewhat structured societal expectations, each other's bodies, the sensations produced by "fooling around," and the delicate timing of good loving—"mutual pleasuring," in the currently fashionable vernacular.

Contrast the 1950ish style of learning about sex, sensuality, and intimacy with the experience of Don, whom we quoted earlier about how much was expected and how quickly. Perhaps this phenomenon is only a sign of the times; one must be ready for anything at any time. Nonetheless, for the adolescent, beset by internal and external confusions and problems to resolve, it seems that a little more structure in the matter of sexual development might be desirable.

It has been my impression that in the past five to ten years or so, many young people are avoiding deeper emotional involvements. There seems to be less going steady or even regular dating, as these concepts were known and practiced by older generations. Today's teenagers appear to take a somewhat "cooler" attitude, as if they were afraid to commit emotionally, to invest a part of themselves in another. To love is, of course, to trust. To trust is to risk. Perhaps today's teens have seen too much unhappiness and bitterness in parental marriages and divorces. Perhaps their attitudes reflect what some feel is the prevailing narcissism of the times. Perhaps they have little to give someone else, being too busy giving to themselves.

These are somewhat gloomy and pessimistic thoughts and they may only reflect my own observations of a limited sampling. There are many young people who seem to have no difficulties at all with relationships of any kind. I am only indicating what seems to be a trend or tendency on the part of

some young people toward emotional distance from others.

I am not alone, however, in some of my observations about these apparent trends in adolescent sexuality. The following are comments of Dr. Herbert Hendin in the journal *Medical Aspects of Human Sexuality* (October, 1978):

> . . . many young people are moving away from emotional involvement. One important kind of defense is to deaden feelings so as not to be moved by passion. They [the young people] are very controlled. Relationships are entered into with narrow expectations, and only a very narrow range of emotions is permitted . . .With the attitude that there is no past and no future to an interpersonal experience, you're not as vulnerable.

Hendin also goes on to make the following very perceptive observation:

> [Many of today's young women] see their mothers [apparently including the emotional involvement they perceive their mothers as having for their spouse] as models for what they do *not* want to be . . . while many of the mothers, more so than I would have imagined, consciously see themselves as models for what they don't want their daughters to be, and let their daughters know that very early on.

As so often is the case in human affairs, the adolescent generation's general lack of commitment to a partner for any length of time, a lack of commitment to a "love relationship," appears to leave them with something gained and something lost. Surely, there is a gain in the movement away from sex as sin and toward sex as natural. But just as surely (and here, I suppose, I reflect somewhat old-fashioned values) something is lost if sex is separated from love and seen as only another form of self-indulgent fun.

Among the swinging singles, generally in the late adolescent phase, who frequent bars and night spots of various "in" locations in Southern California, the term, "sport screwing"

has been coined. This term, it seems to me, is a sad one. On the one hand, it has overtones of Dr. Fred Stoller's ideas, based on his research at UCLA, that agression underlies all sexuality. For another thing, the term seems to state explicitly that the mechanical act of intercourse is the aim, the goal, and the entire meaning of the activity. If this is true, then (as Dr. Stoller said upon concluding his report on human sexual behavior) it is "too bad."

I do not fully agree with Dr. Stoller's conclusions that all human sexuality is based upon deep-seated aggressive tendencies. Rather, I feel that our culture contains so much aggressiveness that almost no activity is free of competition, comparison, and bumps and shoves for advantageous position. But if Stoller's idea is correct, yet we as a society actually do want to foster gentler, more loving, and more lasting *loving* relationships, we must give much more thought to how such relationships are formed and nurtured.

If we, as a society, want certain qualities of humaness fostered, then we, *as a society*, will have to provide full cultural impact to reinforce these qualities. At a minimum, we must consider carefully what our young people are exposed to on television and in print, how best to foster positive intergenerational contact, and how best to help parents and teachers in this vitally important area.

From the standpoint of learning about love (and loving), there are probably no better models for young people than parents who deeply care for each other and show their love toward one another in countless ways. Parents who are comfortable with themselves as people and with their relationship, including the sexual aspects, are simply invaluable resources for their young. Of course it is not necessary for young people to observe their parents "making love" in order for them to observe "good loving." Good loving should always be evident, with proficiency in the technical aspects of sexual lovemaking flowing easily and naturally from proficiency in knowing how people should treat one another in general.

However, there is still a very large place for additional information about sexuality, intimacy, and caring. You as a parent can and should help your young person judge when an individual is being dehumanized, when someone is being treated as an object only, and when one person is being insufficiently sensitive to the needs of another. Such teaching can often take place subtly, using just a comment or two about some behavior or activity that one of you has observed. Assuming your own attitude is reasonably clear on the subject, you might open a discussion about attitudes shown by one person toward another on a TV show, in a movie, or by mutual acquaintances. If *North Dallas Forty* is actually about the violence and brutalization of people within a much-admired and emulated, high-visibility segment of our society (professional football and, by extension, professional sports), do the young people get the point? If not, is someone there to help them get it? Many teenagers, left to their own observations and comprehensional powers, might well see the violence and sexual exploitation in such films as examples to be followed.

If we are to develop civilized sensitivities in our young, we ourselves must have such sensitivities. And we must be able and willing to share them in a nonlecturing, palatable fashion. Generally a word or two will do. Here is a relatively simple educational formula:

a. Help the young person to *discriminate* (become keenly aware of) the behavior in question (for example, the violence, the sexual innuendos and exploitation),

b. Make a simple, straightforward moral/psychological statement, and

c. Offer some constructive alternative(s).

Such a teaching lesson after a violent movie might go as follows between an adult and a young person who had just watched the movie together:

Adult: What do you think of it?

Young person: I like it. What a life those guys have. Smashing each other. All the good-looking babes. Terrific!

Adult: Yeah. Those are exciting, all right. But I don't know about the violence and all. It seems a bit much.

Young person: They get paid for it.

Adult: We sure live in a weird society, don't we? [Now into the discrimination of the behavior.] One that pays people for being violent—sports like football, boxing, even basektball.

Young person: It's exciting. I like it. What's wrong with it?

Adult: Nothing's wrong with it. All of us have a part in us that really likes violence and excitement and wild sex. That's what sells movies like this. We *want* to see and sort of experience all that wild stuff in us. It's just a natural thing, I guess, in all of us. Nothing wrong with the feelings. [Now the moral/psychological statement.] The only way we can judge right or wrong is how we express the feelings. I guess if we are ever to live in a more peaceful and gentle way with each other and have a quieter existence we are going to have to gradually come off so much involvement with this kind of excitement. As for me, I go for sports and for people who play, talk, and live in calmer, more civilized ways. I guess I'd rather flip a frisbee than smash someone with a forearm shiver. As they say, I'd rather talk than fight. I'd rather make love, not war [offering more constructive alternative behaviors].

Young person: Can we stop somewhere for a hamburger?

Adult: Sure, where shall we go?

You, as the adult in this conversation, either have made or failed to make the point. No more need or should be said right now about the subject. To go further would be to move into criticizing something your young person has enjoyed. You have allowed him enjoyment of the sex and violence, indicating that the *feelings* were not wrong but that *behavior* can be judged right or wrong. You then went on to a quick point about ways of living with others, even being specific about behavior ("I'd rather flip a frisbee than smash someone . . .").

The same type of adult teaching technique (discrimination, gentle confrontation, alternatives) can be used for any subject material. From a sexual standpoint, it seems important to keep the focus on how to handle each other gently, with great regard for the other's feelings. The message must be: People are not things, not toys to be felt, poked, then thrown away.

Meaningful relationships with other people are essential to being fully human. Our young need much assistance in coming to an understanding of this.

CHAPTER 11

Reality: Coming to Terms with the "Nitty-gritty" of Daily Life

I didn't remind my children of deadlines such as for the SAT application or for college applications. When they were seniors in high school, I would not even attend parent conferences. I told my children and the school that if they could not work out any problems which arose between them, it was not likely that I could help, either. I figured if my kids weren't mature enough to get themselves through high school and into college, maybe they shouldn't be in college and should still be in high school.

A middle-aged parent

Know what I like about sports? There's no bull. You can either do it or you can't. Just about every place else in my life I can lie, to others, to myself. But if you kid yourself in sports, you're doomed.

A teen-age athlete

We parents tend to protect our young from the hard knocks of daily life. We write the "white lie" excuse for school. We intervene if another child is bullying our child. We argue with the Little League coach for more playing time for our child. We help with homework. The list could go on and on. The point is, most parents tend to do a lot for their kids. Perhaps too much.

At some point, one has to begin assuming responsibility for one's own behavior. We can't learn about the reality of the

world if we are constantly shielded from the consequences of our actions. Parents who overprotect their children may in fact be clipping their wings and hampering their growth of independence in thought and action.

Experience is a very good teacher. Yet as parents we seem too often to go counter to the wisdom of that statement. Perhaps it is because we remember the pains of our own adolescence and, out of love, hope to absorb some of the heartaches and guard our offspring from them. But in child raising sometimes "less is more." The good parent has to know when to step back, when to turn over the reins of responsibility to the young person. Zero risks, low stresses, and many buffers between actions and their consequences, impair development. Sometimes it is a valuable lesson if the teenager simply makes a mistake, loses a job, blows a school assignment, or gets kicked off a team for irresponsibility.

There are some exceptions to this, although I hesitate to suggest any at all. However, one exception might be a severely psychologically disturbed youngster whose reality confrontations might lead to physical harm coming to such a youngster or others. So while each situation must be taken on its individual merits, the basic idea still stands—parents must allow reality confrontations. It is through such confrontations that the young person's character and reality orientation are formed.

The parents in a family I was working with had, as the father termed it, "put up with a lot of teen-age bull" from their adolescent children. Finally the parents reached some definite conclusions about how things ought to go in their home. This new stance developed out of much professional counseling, in which one of the essential questions revolved around the extend of their parental responsibilities and how far they were willing to go in letting their adolescent children dictate how the family and the household would be run. One evening, in my office, the father announced to his startled 17-year-old son and 18-year-old daughter:

> We can't go on living the way we are living together. It's no good for any of us. You kids don't respect your mother or me, and we are coming to hold very deep resentments toward you. Whether you like certain rules and regulations or not, we are going to have them, and what's more, we are all going to treat each other like normal, civilized people.

The father then went on to spell out certain very simple, rudimentary rules, such as telephoning home if plans change, no smoking pot or having pot paraphernalia in the house, cleaning up after themselves in the den and kitchen and other common living areas of the home, and showing simple courtesy toward one another.

In dealing with children or adolescents it is especially important to heed the old maxim, "Say what you mean and mean what you say." The parents had carefully thought through how they wanted their family to live, what they wanted to say about it, and how far they would go to insist upon retaining the kind of structure they had decided was important in their lives and the lives of their children. The father's concluding remarks indicate how far he was prepared to go:

> If you kids feel that these demands are silly or unreasonable, so be it. When you have a home of your own and children of your own, you will structure things as you see fit. Meanwhile, you live here with your mother and me and we live here with you. Let me remind you that this is a pretty nice hotel. Good food, clean clothes, a swimming pool, color TV, and no particular work demands. So, you may not like us or the rules I have just laid down, but you do have to abide by them as long as you live under this roof. If you feel you cannot or will not abide by the rules, then you will have to look for another hotel.

Perhaps this seems like a very hard statement. But to me it was a reality confrontation that made good sense. The parents

really meant what they said. If they had been tentative or unsure of their ground, likely to give in once more or be steamrollered once again by their teenagers, then the confrontation would have been counterproductive. In that case, they would have been presenting their teenagers with a reality which, in effect, said that rules are not rules, structure can be bent, and words are only words. When this message is sent, and adolescents generalize this perception of reality to the world outside the family, they are likely to suffer damage in one form or another.

The reaction of these particular teenagers was interesting. Initially, both of them perceived their father's statement as meaning they were being "thrown out of the house." This distortion was discussed and resolved. The young people then argued that the rules were "too hard and too unrealistic." Whether requesting civil behavior in one's home was "hard" or "unrealistic" was then discussed (with the aid of the counselor) and resolved. Months later, a follow-up call from me found all members of the family living together with respect for each other's rights and in reasonable friendship.

Out of what depths of insecurity are so many parents ruled by or overruled by their children? What, basically, do we "owe" our children? And, ultimately, is it helpful to them for parents to always give in, to put their children's desires first and foremost, or to fail to offer strong structure and guidance in important matters involving how to treat one another in a civil manner?

These of course are questions that each of us must examine carefully and answer according to one's own individual attitudes and goals. But they are questions which, for the sake of our young people, we cannot ignore.

My strong recommendation is that you *not* always give in, *not* always put your child's desires first, and *not* always overshield your teenager from the consequences of his behavior.

What is or is not overshield is obviously a value judgment, but many instances seem clear. To do your young person's homework serves no useful purpose. You probably would

agree with this (assuming you agree that homework has some value in the first place). Nor can you help your youngster learn how to do such things as carpentry, rock climbing, or construction of computer circuitry by doing them yourself. The art appears to be in knowing how to help a person get started and then bowing out in a graceful and inconspicuous manner as quickly as possible. It is difficult to teach someone such an art and about all I can do in that direction is to provide you with information about adolescence. You then must apply the concepts as you perceive them and as they fit your own situation.

Many of us try to control our teenagers and to teach them about the "real world" by scolding, nagging, arguing, yelling, grounding, and the like. I believe there is a better way, and it is the *if-then contingency statement*, which was used by the parents in our earlier example. In this technique, a parent simply states the contingencies in advance, then later acts upon them. ("*If* you do this, *then* this is going to happen.") When possible, put the statement in a positive form rather than negative. For example, "If your grades are all passing on the midterm report, then you may continue to have the privilege of television during the week and going out on weekends." What you are saying to your teenager is that what happens or does not happen is your teenager's responsibility, not yours. Taking responsibility for our own behavior is hard. It is *so* easy to tend to blame someone else. If-then statements are obviously excellent reality teachers. Their main purpose is two-fold: (1) to state the limits in advance rather than meting out some unannounced and arbitrary punishment after the fact, and (2) to toss the responsibility of the young person's behavior squarely where it belongs—with the young person.

When you make such a statement to your teenager, the contingencies are clear. The implication is that failure to comply will mean suspension of privileges.

However, you have not made the scene heavy and negative or presented yourself as a mean, punitive parent. You have

merely placed the responsibility for *future* events (watching TV or going out on weekends), directly upon *current* behavior (studying enough to obtain a passing grade). Losses for transgressions will not be your responsibility, but the transgressor's.

When you are using this very powerful technique, you have to think carefully through what you want from the young person, what you are trying to teach and/or guard against, and whether or not you can and will actually hold to the statement.

For instance, parents of my acquaintance used an if-then contingency with their teen-age daughter over whether or not she would be able to attend sleep-away camp. But the parents had planned their vacation around the assumption that she would be in camp during that particular time in summer. When the daughter, for some infraction or other, goofed on the contingencies laid down by the parents, they were left in the position of either having to take her with them on their vacation, cancel their vacation, or go back on their statement and send her off to camp anyway. The parents had put themselves in a no-win situation by not carefully thinking through what they were saying and whether they really meant it.

By all means avoid using the if-then contingency statement if you cannot follow through on the terms. And remember that it is not primarily a punitive technique. There may be a punishment involved in the sense that some desirable outcome is not forthcoming or some privilege is lost, but the critical point is that this happens because of the young person's behavior, rather than because of an arbitrary whim on your part.

Since the real world largely functions within if-then contingencies (if I don't come to work, I won't get paid; if I run a red light, I'm likely to get a traffic ticket; if I am an insulting boor, I may not be reinvited to my host's home), we adults do well to provide training for our young people within such contingency frameworks.

CHAPTER 12

Drugs

At my school there are the surfers, the jocks, the dopers, and the turkeys. If you aren't a surfer or jock, it's easy to drift into the doper group. At least it's better than being a turkey.

A 16-year-old high school boy in West Los Angeles

From approximately the 1960s on, our young people have been exposed to drugs and/or involved with them on a wider, deeper scale than probably any previous generation.

It is a fact of modern life in western civilization that we exist in a chemically oriented society. Drug use of one kind or another is everywhere. We are conditioned from early in life to use pills for pain and to use other drugs such as nicotine, caffeine, and alcohol for relaxation and as aids to social interaction.

The modern young have added marijuana to our society's common drug list. And other drugs, such as Quaaludes, Valium, cocaine, speed in various forms, and LSD, while less frequently used than marijuana, are not uncommon enough to cause much comment or concern among young people.

Many adults are now conditioned to the use of marijuana by their youngsters. In fact, many adults use marijuana themselves. Perhaps you personally are in agreement with the so-called decriminalization laws that have been passed in various states making the possession of small amounts of marijuana for personal use a "crime" for citation only, of

about the magnitude of a traffic ticket. Adult attitudes toward pills or other harder drugs, however, are often still highly negative.

There is a good reason why this brief chapter on drugs follows on the heels of the chapter on reality. It is my contention that *anything* that interferes with reality confrontations between the adolescent and the environment also hinders development of adequate reality ties and adequate coping behavior. This in turn impairs the development of basic feelings of self-worth.

Obviously, other factors can also interfere with reality confrontation. Children, as well as adults, often fall back on psychological defenses such as repression and denial to ward off the hard blows of reality. We project, displace, pretend, and fantasize. The human mind is uniquely capable of distorting things. Some people strongly need to view the world through rose-colored glasses and to see things as they want or need to see them. Other people seem consistently to perceive things on a pessimistic note, seeing the glass half empty instead of half full. Most of us fall somewhere in between these extremes. By now all of this is rather old hat in today's psychologicaly sophisticated society.

We have already talked about how as a parent you may feel the desire to screen your child from "harsh reality." While your concern may show how much you care, being overprotective can also send out the hidden message that you do not have much confidence in your child's ability to resolve the various problem situations of life without help. It is said that if a chick is not allowed to peck itself out of the egg, it will be weak and sickly and less likely to survive. This seems a likely result, psychologically speaking, for young humans as well.

We must *dare* something in assisting the development of our young. Perhaps we must risk our children's failures or mistakes in order to help them be stronger later. They do not learn how to deal with the complexities and stresses of life if we instead of they always deal with them. As with so many

things in life, on-the-job training seems to be the best teacher.

Unfortunately, this present adolescent generation has added drugs to the other two major reality buffers—psychological defenses and parental protection. The principal reason that people of any age use the major social drugs is to alter mood, change frame of mind, decrease anxiety, and relax. Nicotine, caffeine, alcohol, and marijuana are currently used by large segments of our population, sometimes frequently and often at fairly high dosage levels.

Because we as a society are so desensitized to drug use, and because we adults have been so unsuccessful in preventing drug use by our young, we are not as concerned as we should be about the possible harmful effects of certain drugs on our young people. We show deep concern only when the thing we fear seems out of control.

I for one feel alarmed at the complacency of so many parents about their children's drug use, especially when the children are in those extremely critical transformation years between puberty and approximately middle-adolescence. I believe that even the *moderate* us of drugs *of any sort* during that age hampers psychological development in a number of ways, has negative physiological effects, and may have long-term negative consequences in both intellectual and emotional growth.

Therefore, I feel I cannot stress too strongly that *any* substance that blurs your adolescent's reality, alters brain functioning as well as moods, and fosters withdrawal from learning to deal with the general stress of life, can seriously impair the capacity to cope effectively with the problems of daily living. Additionally, the great transitional problems of adolescence—the move from childhood to adulthood, the changes in logical thinking, the considerations of later independence, and the development of the ability to grapple with a changing world— are all masked and confused by the quick anxiety reduction offered by drugs such as marijuana and alcohol, not to mention the "heavy duty" drugs such as PCP, LSD, and heroin.

Ideally, young people from puberty to middle-adolescence should use no drugs at all except under medical direction. We seem to recognize intuitively the bad effects of drugs on our young people when we admonish them against smoking cigarettes and drinking coffee (because they "stunt your growth"). And we distinctly look askance at the consumption of alcohol by children and adolescents, although we generally begin to relax all of these prohibitions during middle- and late-adolescence.

But despite our intuitive feelings about drug use by our children, many young people today begin smoking marijuana during early adolescence, often starting even before puberty in late childhood!

Worse is the fact that for the youngsters in their early teens, the smoking of marijuana seems to become almost obsessive-compulsive. These young people spend more time thinking and talking about pot than about any other subject, including sex! Furthermore, they do not stop at just thinking and talking. Many of them smoke moderately to heavily, with "moderately" being defined as three to five joints (marijuana cigarettes) per week, smoked on separate occasions, and "heavily" defined as five or more joints per week, or virtually daily use. These are, of course, arbitrary definitions but in general they agree with the thinking of the young people I have known. A boy of 14 states:

> I just smoke "recreationally," like at a party on the weekend. Maybe a joint or two. Sometimes I'll take a "hit" [drag] from a friend during the week. But it's no big deal. Some of my friends, though, really smoke out, like every day. A person smoking every day, yeah, that would be heavy smoking. Keep on with that, they just become "fried" [they fry their brain], can't think and can't do. They're just "veges" [vegetables] when they get going that much, usually using the heavy stuff [strong marijuana], too.

As in the 1960s, when young people came to know more about various drugs and made keener distinctions in terms of potential harmfulness of one drug versus another, the adoles-

cents of today tend to differentiate recreational use of marijuana from heavy duty use. Also, today's teenagers tend to
view marijuana as a light (i.e., nonharmful) drug as opposed
to heavy drugs such as heroin, PCP, or LSD. In my experience, a great many young people are also coming to view
cocaine, codeine, and drugs such as Quaaludes as falling
somewhere between light and heavy on the drug scale. The
occasional use of any of these drugs, alone or in combination,
is viewed as no "biggie," one way or the other.

Humankind's age-old companion, alcohol, is not ignored
by today's young people. In fact, teen drinking appears to be
on the upsurge, after suffering reduced popularity for some
years. The California State Psychological Association's
newsletter notes that:

> An estimated 3.3 million youngsters aged 14 to 17 are
> considered problem drinkers, or nearly one-fifth of
> teenagers. The young people's problems tend to be acute
> rather than chronic and involve binge drinking.

Many teenagers of my acquaintance say that if alcoholic
beverages were as easy to obtain or conceal as pot, they
would drink rather than smoke marijuana. It is difficult to
conceal a bottle of wine in one's shirt or blouse, whereas it is
quite easy to conceal an ounce of marijuana.

Any discussion of the modern adolescent is incomplete
without a reasonably thorough and in-depth review of the "pot
phenomenon"—the general use of marijuana, the drug of the
young. A *Newsweek* article titled "The New Bootleggers" states:

> In effect, pot smugglers have become the contemporary
> equivalent of Prohibition-era bootleggers, serving a
> huge market. Forty million Americans have smoked
> marijuana at least once, and eleven states have
> eliminated criminal penalties for possession of small
> amounts. *"It's pretty impossible nowadays to hit 15
> without smoking a joint,"* [italics added] sighs Lt. John
> Hinchy of the Chicago vice-control division.
>
> **"Condensed from Newsweek" (by permission).**

The next chapter is devoted to a review of current research findings on the effects of marijuana on the human body. Some of this research is from a very pro-pot source: Ms. Pamela Lloyd, former executive editor of the marijuana "bible," *High Times*. One reason I quote from Ms. Lloyd is to demonstrate to young people reading this book that I am not simply one more stick-in-the-mud adult who reacts negatively to pot no matter what. I do react negatively to pot for adolescents, but my reaction is based on what I consider to be good evidence. And I shall present this evidence in the form of summaries of research from noted investigators, clinical findings, and updated statements from those involved in the argument about young people and marijuana.

An initial, sensible step for you and any other adult who is involved with adolescents is to take the trouble to become reasonably well informed about the various drugs of the young. For one thing, you should know some of the basic symptoms of drug use. The slurred speech and uncertain coordination of the person under the influence of alcohol is already well-known to most people. The hyperactive, fast-talking, lip-licking behavior of the person involved with some amphetamine-type drug (an "upper") is easily recognized. The red-eyed look, sleeping, and voracious eating habits of the marijuana smoker have become increasingly well known to many parents and teachers (though many teenagers counter part of the symptoms with eyewash and learn to "maintain" very well through an ordinary conversation or in a classroom situation).

The symptoms of drug overdose may be unfamiliar to you but are important for you to recognize. For this reason I am including at the end of this chapter a section listing common overdose symptoms and suggestions for emergency actions you can take.

Let us return to a less dire kind of situation. Let's say that your kids use drugs (or you suspect they do), but they still function adequately in school and elsewhere as far as you can tell. What should you do? You should react immediately. But

you should not overreact. Most teenagers using drugs are not addicts and are not heading down the road to hell in a wheelbarrow. But you should not waste any time before taking the following steps:

1. Take a strong antidrug stand. Let it be known that you are completely against the use of drugs of any kind as far as your youngsters are concerned.

2. State that there will be no pot smoking or other drug use in your house. Say further that there will be definite penalties such as grounding, restrictions from certain peers, and so on. (Remember now, we are talking about children around the age of puberty or early adolescence—you really do still exercise some control at these ages. For the good of your children, you must not be afraid to use this control.)

I realize that you cannot control all your children's behavior or that of their friends. But you would have to be wearing blinders not to notice that doors are more frequently closed, homework assignments are not being handed in, and your teenager often looks and acts like a zombie from the late show. At that point, you have to react. But that does not mean you must have a tantrum and throw the kid out in the street or use physical violence. To react means to discuss, and to continue your course of action.

3. Make all *credible* information possible available to your children. Scare pamphlets or talks do not work. You have to have hard data and present it well. If you feel that you can't do this, then get together with some other parents and invite a qualified speaker to your school. Some parents organize rap groups in which more communication between parents and teenagers is attempted. In these sessions, drug use (or abuse) is a highly relevant topic. Again, both parents and teenagers usually respect a reasonably neutral authority. It also seems likely to me that a Pamela Lloyd or some other very promarijuana *adult* could speak very effectively to young people about the dangers of overuse during the early teen years. For the most part, adult pot advocates such as Pamela Lloyd are not wild-eyed fanatics. They just forget sometimes, or have

never considered, how complicated adolescence really is, and how much more messed up a kid can get with a bunch of junk floating around in the brain cells, shorting out the synapses.

Another way of getting information is to make an appointment with a knowledgeable child-guidance professional for an in-depth discussion on drugs of all sorts. Prior to setting such an appointment, however, I would ascertain the professional's attitude about different drugs. Some counselors specializing with adolescents tend to be "soft" on pot. I believe you cannot afford a soft attitude toward pot or any other drug not medically prescribed for good reason.

4. If none of the steps above seem to have the desired effect and your child is evidently becoming increasingly drug-involved, seek counseling assistance from a qualified and experienced professional. Such assistance might involve the young person alone and/or family members, as the counselor feels appropriate.

5. If the counselor forgets to do so, explore the possibilities of a school transfer for your child if it seems that part of the problem is that he or she is attending a highly drug-oriented school. Knowledgeable educators know that some schools are more "druggy" than others. They will often tell you if you ask, though they will only speak off the record.

6. For the middle- or older-adolescent, if none of the above steps work and you cannot control the addiction, seek professional advice about the possibility of a residential treatment center. Placing a young person in a drug rehabilitation center is a very large step and must be done only with extreme caution. You should only go that far if you feel that your teenager is in danger of overdosing and committing suicide, or if you feel that there is danger to other members of the family, such as younger brothers or sisters, who are exposed to the teenager's drug use.

7. Never, never, never relent in your antidrug attitude. You wouldn't want your children to look back in later life and say they received any mixed messages from you about drug use. Your consistent message should be: Don't use drugs!

In summary, don't be afraid to lock horns with your teenager over the drug issue. In a way, you have nothing to lose and everything to gain. At the worst, your child may run away from home because of your "old-fashioned" attitude. Usually the child will come home quite quickly (having spent a few nights with a friend), and you as a parent will have gained something in that you have made your moral position clear on this issue. You held fast for your child's sake. You did not support, by failure to act, an undermining habit that could seriously impair your child. And your firmness and ability to say no is also helpful in other ways, as we shall see later.

If your teenager is involved in moderate to heavy drug use, there is always the possibility of an inadvertent overdose. You should always call a physician if you suspect your child has overdosed on drugs, but in the meantime you may be able to take helpful action yourself.

Guidelines for Common Overdoses

A drug overdose comes about when a drug (or several drugs) has been ingested in such a quantity that the individual's physical tolerance level has been exceeded. In general, the degree of danger involved depends on the drug and the amount taken. Tolerance level for any drug also depends upon factors such as body size, whether one is accustomed to taking the drug or not, general health, allergenic reactions to a particular drug, and general mood or state of mind at the time of ingestion. Also, the way a drug acts on an individual depends, often in large part, on whether that person has also taken other drugs. When two or more drugs are taken at nearly the same time, drug interaction effects have to be considered.

A great many teenagers do not seem well aware of the potential dangers involved in drug interactions. Many young people with whom I have talked have actually been surprised to learn that mixing alcohol with almost any other drug can be potentially very dangerous. The use of alcohol and marijuana is common, as is alcohol and Quaaludes. The users of

such combinations either do not know or do not care about the potential ill effects of such combinations. For either teenagers or parents who care, however, an excellent chapter on the interaction effects of both prescribed and nonprescribed drugs may be found in Joe Graedon's book, *The People's Pharmacy*.

Today's teenagers talk glibly about "uppers," "downers," "hash," "acid," "ludes," and so on. This brief section cannot go into the effects of all drugs and the symptoms associated with overdoses of the various drugs (or drug interactions). However, this section will give you some idea about what to watch for and what to do if your teenager has taken too much of some drug. But if things look scary, if the young person has passed out, for example, don't waste time looking through this or any other book. Call a doctor fast!

With that said, let's take a quick and somewhat unpleasant look at some of the drugs and symptoms involved in common overdoses, while also offering suggestions about what to do while awaiting medical help.

UPPERS

"Uppers" are stimulant drugs such as amphetamines, Ritalin, cocaine, and caffeine. Symptoms associated with an overdose of one or more of these drugs are:

1. Excitement, restlessness, agitation
2. Breathing rapidly (hungry for air)
3. Pulse feels pounding and rapid
4. Visible pulsations in head
5. Skin hot and flushed, lips dark
6. Hand and arm tremors
7. Generalized shaking
8. May be confused

Until medical help arrives, take the following action:

1. Sit person up
2. Encourage person to take deep breaths calmly through mouth
3. Give fluids, preferably warm

4. If person begins to faint, have any breathing difficulty, become hot to the touch, or have convulsions, rush to emergency hospital

DOWNERS

"Downers" are depressant drugs such as alcohol, sedatives such as Quaaludes or sleeping pills, opiates, and barbiturates. Some of the symptoms associated with an overdose of a downer drug are:

1. Difficulty in arousing the individual
2. Breathing not effective
3. Hands and arms cold and moist
4. Bluish fingernails, lips, and gums

These symptoms indicate the need for artificial respiration and a call for medical help. If a physician cannot come to you, take your teenager to a hospital equipped with an emergency room. When you get there, the youngster, if conscious, will be given a substance (Ipecac) to cause vomiting, or if unconscious, his or her stomach will be pumped.

OTHER BAD STUFF

Teenagers (and others) have been known to ingest drugs such as belladonna, alkaloids, atropine, Jimson Weed, Sominex, Compoz, Quiet World, San Man, Sleep-Eze, Donnatal, strychnine, and others. Some youngsters sniff airplane glue, eat mushrooms, or take LSD ("acid"). If your teenager manifests difficulty in talking or swallowing, very large pupils, a flushed, hot red face, dry mouth, blurred vision— with these symptoms accompanied by a fever—then get medical help fast!

If you know that an individual has taken belladonna, alert medical personnel quickly because oxygen may be needed and a determination of blood gas levels must be made.

When in doubt, don't wait. Take your teenager to an emergency hospital or call your physician. In these days, believe it or not, most emergency hospitals do not consider the "common overdose" any big deal. So don't be embar-

rassed. Get the kid in there fast and get the junk out. In general, if you don't mention suicide and you say that the drug was taken by "mistake," the police don't have to be involved. If you are lucky enough to get away with a stomach-pumping and your child is still alive, you should, in any case, seek professional counseling assistance from someone who is experienced in dealing with the stresses and strains on young people. In short, call a qualified psychotherapist at once: a psychologist, a psychiatrist, or a psychiatric social worker.

CHAPTER 13

Marijuana

When I'm eighteen I'm splitting for Oregon. My folks can shove it. There are big farms up there where they grow marijuana. You get paid off in hash and you sell some of it for food and get stoned royally on the rest. That's what I want to do with my life.
A 17-year-old doper who is breaking his parents' hearts

Any book about today's teenagers has to talk about marijuana, the main drug of the young. As parents, we continue to hear conflicting stories about marijuana. Some say that it is bad, but not as dangerous as cocaine or heroin—or even alcohol. Others, especially young people, claim that marijuana is similar to alcohol and if adults can sip cocktails how harmful is it for teenagers to smoke joints? Some respected researchers tell us that marijuana is an innocent drug. Other researchers disagree, stating that marijuana has highly negative effects on the brain and body.

What is the truth? Whom are we to believe? Is there anyone without an axe to grind on one side or the other?

Contrary to what many people seem to think, there is a great deal of good marijuana research, and I could devote an entire book just to summarizing it. But since this is not a book primarily about drugs, I would like to summarize only some of the more recent information. This will include research by people who initially felt that marijuana was a relatively mild or harmless drug and who later changed their minds. I will also quote Ms. Pamela Lloyd, the former executive editor of

High Times and author of *Pot*, a book considered by some to be the definitive work on marijuana. Her comments range from the historical use of pot over the centuries to the chemistry of marijuana to, finally, instructions on how to choose, smoke, eat, and grow "weed." *Pot* is very much a promarijuana-use book, so I use it as a balance to the anti-marijuana research findings. Both parents and teenagers should find all this quite interesting. I know I do.

Since so many teenagers use the argument that pot is no better and no worse than alcohol, and that the two drugs are similar, let's begin with a quick comment on that point of view. As you will see after reading this chapter, the argument that marijuana and alcohol are similar drugs just doesn't hold up. Certainly alcohol does qualify as a drug, just as marijuana does. Both drugs alter the user's mood and state of consciousness, affect coordination and judgment, are psychologically and physically addictive, and can have seriously harmful effects on various body organs, especially the brain. There are, however, very important differences. Marijuana and alcohol are quite dissimilar in their chemical makeup and in the *way* they affect the mind and other parts of the body. Of course in talking about the effects of any drug, it is important to consider the frequency of use and dosage level. Another extremely important consideration that appears somewhat underappreciated by many drug researchers and others is the age at which the drug use begins. The younger the person, the more the potential danger from drug use. The indications that our children are beginning to use marijuana and other drugs at younger and younger ages is particularly ominous.

Ms. Lloyd offers an instructive overview of pot. She tells us that R. Adams isolated and identified the cannabis compound tetrahydrocannabinol (THC) as the substance largely responsible for the marijuana "high" and that insufficient research has been conducted since, considering the importance of the area. She notes that both the Food and Drug Administration and the Drug Enforcement Administration

have tended to be roadblocks to scientific experiments with marijuana. She also explains that the few researchers who have managed to initiate research on the effects of marijuana have never established a "standard dose" of·marijuana or, more importantly, the amount of THC in it. Obviously, without such a standard dosage level, meaningful comparisons between research efforts are difficult if not impossible. For this reason, she does not include a review of the research literature to any significant extent.

I must pause to mention two facts, which we will discuss further later. First, despite various research difficulties in the past, there is now an increasing body of important research findings. Second, psychotherapists who specialize with adolescents have discovered a great deal about the correlation of marijuana use and psychic turmoil among their teenage patients.

Now let us continue with Ms. Lloyd, since she is a splendid introductory guide. Lloyd notes that THC occurs naturally only in the cannabis plant. The resins and dried foliage of the plant are known as pot or marijuana. The solidified resin on the plant is called hashish or "hash." Cannabis can be eaten or smoked. The inhaled high can take effect within five minutes, usually peaking within the hour. The ingested high comes on within ninety minutes and peaks between one and three hours after ingestion, depending upon the speed of the person's digestion. Lloyd notes that hash can contain eight times as much THC as the grass from which it was extracted.

According to Lloyd, "Within five minutes of smoking half a joint, the smoker's heart rate increases from average, about 80 beats a minute, to upwards of 100. The heart rate continues to increase for about 15 minutes, then begins to return to normal" (p. 37). She goes on to note that pot can act as either a stimulant or a depressant to the central nervous system and that the drug has been useful in the treatment of asthma, glaucoma, and the relief of vomiting in cancer patients. However, it is currently illegal for physicians to prescribe cannabis for medical purposes.

As another aside, a number of physicians of my acquaintance have told me that they have, in fact, suggested the use of marijuana to some of their hypertense and overwrought patients for whom the more usual medical prescription might be Valium or some other mild tranquilizer. Whether this is good medicine or not remains to be seen. Recently, also, a number of studies and informal reports have surfaced pointing out negative side effects of marijuana used as a medically prescribed agent. It seems there are other drugs available that can do the job better than marijuana and without the side effects.

Lloyd's description of other physical reactions to marijuana cannot be improved upon, and I quote her:

> In addition to acting as a stimulant and a depressant at different times, even simultaneously, throughout the duration of its effects, cannabis causes a slight rise in blood pressure initially, tremor and vertigo (dizziness) in some cases, slight ataxia (impaired muscular coordination), hyperreflexia, increased tactile sensitivity, and a marked increase in appetite, a condition popularly known as "the munchies." Cannabis also has a hypothermic effect, chilling the subject's extremities, and causes "dry mouth," thirstiness. The most obvious tip-off that a person is high from pot is injection of the conjunctivae, reddening of the eyes. Dilation of the pupils, an effect associated with several other drugs, does *not* [italics added] occur with the cannabis high. (p. 38)

Before we continue with Lloyd's description of the psychological effects of marijuana, let us broaden our discussion of the physical effects.

Dr. Harold Kolansky and Dr. William Moore, of the Department of Psychiatry, University of Pennsylvania School of Medicine, after considerable work and thought on the matter, have arrived at the conclusion that marijuana is not a mild and innocuous drug. These doctors feel that marijuana is a habit-forming drug with various toxic qualities.

Further, they feel that the public is poorly informed about some of the more harmful effects of the use of marijuana.

Kolansky and Moore, in the *Journal of the American Medical Association*, write as follows:

> In our reports, we detailed the toxic psychological effects of cannabis use in 51 of our patients, all of whom demonstrated symptoms that simultaneously began with cannabis use and disappeared within 3 to 24 months after cessation of drug use. *Moreover, a correlation of the symptoms to the duration and frequency of smoking was established* [italics theirs]. When these observations were coupled with the stereotyped nature of the symptoms seen, regardless of psychological predisposition, we presumed that with intensive cannabis use, biochemical and structural changes occured in the central nervous system. All subjects clearly demonstrated an early *diminution in self-awareness and judgment along with slowed thinking and shorter spans in concentration and attention.* We also reported a gradual development of *goallessness; blunted emotions, a counterfeit impression of calm and well-being, and a prevailing illusion of recently developed insight and emotional maturity. Many demonstrated difficulty in depth perception and an alteration in the sense of timing,* both of which are particularly hazardous during automobile driving. These clinical findings, along with other more severe mental symptoms, have been similarly reported by other investigators.

Kolansky and Moore go on to underscore the point that despite repeated medical warnings regarding the possible toxic effects of the drug, marijuana use appears to continue to escalate. This certainly jibes with my own observations. In my practice, as with the practices of my colleagues, the escalation in marijuana use is not only in sheer numbers, but involves an increase in the number of *pre-teens* experimenting with the drug.

Now, as Pamela Lloyd has noted, the research on marijuana cannot simply be uncritically accepted. As in all research involving complex processes within the human

being, it takes many studies by many researchers, as well as replications of such studies, in order to begin to grope toward some scientific understanding of the phenomena under study. There is little question that the last word in research on marijuana is still a long way off. This is partly due to the difficulties of research on human subjects (you don't just "sacrifice" a human subject after exposure to X amount of marijuana and then observe brain changes, for instance). It is partly due to the slowness of researchers to agree on a standard THC dose, rather than the *amount* of marijuana smoked or ingested. And it is partly due to the tremendous emotional connotations attached to pro or con marijuana statements.

Psychiatrist D. Harvey Powelson, Director of the Student Psychiatric Clinic at the University of California, Berkeley, ran into a good deal of flak upon shifting from a promarijuana to an antimarijuana position. Powelson's clinical observations gradually led him to abandon his original view that the drug is not harmful and ultimately arrive at the conclusion that marijuana smoking causes long-range deleterious effects, including impairment of what he termed a "central organizing principle" in the thinking of the user. In a recent paper Dr. Powelson notes, "It is an interesting fact that questioning the claims of marijuana users leads to much more anger, vilification, and character assassination than does the opposite stance."

Many young people have found it difficult to believe the antimarijuana "propaganda" poured out by parents, educators, and physicians. But the reverse point of view, that marijuana is a simple and benign drug, becomes just as dubious as clinical and laboratory data accumulate. Perhaps, as with politics and religion, everyone believes what he wants to believe about the effects of marijuana. The users want to see "no problem." So, like ostriches, with their heads in smoke instead of sand, they see no problem. On the other hand, some members of the older generation, particularly parents and educators, are in a virtual state of panic about drugs in general and marijuana particularly.

With Dr. Hardin Jones's assistance, let us continue to investigate the evidence about marijuana. Writing in the journal *Executive Health**, Jones makes many important observations:

> For more than a decade, we have been subjected to a flood of articles, books, and reports supporting the idea that smoking marijuana is simply fun and has no serious consequences. Earlier observations that marijuana was linked to mental disorders, to the use of narcotics, and to personality changes have been declared "obsolete" or "exaggerated." *That these early observations are now supported by scientific studies and that many of the early studies were carefully conducted have been ignored* [italics his].
>
> There are problems with many of the reports supporting the harmlessness of marijuana. First, examinations of marijuana smokers early in their use do not reveal the long-term effects. Second, as marijuana causes adverse behavioral changes that the user cannot recognize in himself, some investigators may have been deceived by their own experiences with the drug. Because they cannot feel the ill effects themselves, many investigators have assumed that marijuana would turn out to be as free of long-term effects as most well-tested medicines.
>
> Throughout the same period that the promarijuana reports were being published, the World Health Organization has continued to warn against the use of marijuana. Although some promarijuana inquiries in the past were sponsored by the British and Canadian governments, these governments have since issued clear (negative) warnings about marijuana.

*The editorial board of this journal consists of three Nobel Laureates—Sir Hans Krebs (Physiology and Medicine), Dr. Albert Szent-Gyorgye (Physiology and Medicine) and Dr. Linus Pauling (Chemistry and Peace)—as well as Dr. Hans Selye of the International Institute of Stress, University of Montreal, Dr. Mark Altschule, Professor of Medicine at Harvard and Yale, and Dr. John Stirling Meyer, Professor of Neurology at Baylor University, and various other very distinguished scientists. Such a clearly first-rate editorial board would be expected to demand a high level of research and scholarship in articles appearing in its publication. Dr. Jones's comments, quoted at length in this text, must be taken seriously whether or not all current evidence holds up ultimately.

Jones feel that the effect of marijuana is probably never transitory. He says:

> Marijuana is an unusual drug in that the active ingre-
> dient, *tetrahydrocannabinol* (THC), is retained in the
> body for long periods of time. From animal studies it
> appears that some thirty (30) per cent of the THC from
> marijuana smoking (or eating) is retained in the body at
> the end of a week. Further, the 30 per cent retained at
> the end of a week is eliminated much more slowly than
> the first 70 per cent.

Consequently, with continued smoking or eating of the drug, THC accumulates in the body, And since THC is highly fat-soluble, it is deposited in the fatty outer membrane of cells. Jones states that "THC appears to have adverse effects on all body cells, but there is reason to be especially concerned about its effect on brain cells and on the reproductive process."

Jones goes on to discuss the work of other researchers in this field. He reports on the work of W.D.M. Paton at Oxford University and Robert Heath at Tulane University and their colleagues, who demonstrated profound changes in the surface membranes of brain cells in animals exposed to doses of marijuana within the range of typical human doses. Marijuana seems to injure the fine, hairlike extensions of the brain cells which communicate with other brain cells. Such damage is critical, for these are the mechanisms of the mind.

Researchers have found that THC lingers in human tissues for as long as eight days, particularly in the brain and testicles. It has also been reported that the sperm counts and testosterone levels of their marijuana-using subjects were lowered to the point of temporary infertility in some cases. Other researchers report similarly frightening results from steady marijuana use, affecting the body's immune system and DNA and RHA synthesis. They also report such damage as cells with broken chromosomes, as well as premalignant lesions in lung tissues.

Regarding lung damage, Jones points out that the lungs of

the pot smoker become even more irritated than those of the cigarette smoker. The irritation is greater because the THC is more tightly bound to the carbon particles in the smoke than nicotine is, and in order to get the drug's full effect, the pot smoker must inhale deeply and hold the smoke longer.

It seems very clear to me from these reports that pot is bad for the brain, the lungs, and the reproductive system.

Many marijuana users argue that as bad as marijuana may be, it is not as harmful a drug as alcohol. Young people like to point out to their drinking parents that their own use of marijuana does not seem to lead to problems as serious as the parents' use of alcohol does. Their argument is that marijuana is the alcohol of the young, cheaper and easier to obtain (they can even grow their own) and less harmful. Its principal drawback is that it is illegal.

There is no arguing that a major difference between the two drugs is that alcohol is legal for an adult and marijuana is not. However, various states have decriminalized the possession of marijuana for adults, and more may move along this route in the future. The point that many young people appear to miss is that for *them*, since they are under legal age, both marijuana and alcohol are equally illegal (as I believe they should be). Theoretically, a youngster should be in as much trouble for using one drug as the other. But this is often not what happens. In general, teen-age marijuana smoking has been more stringently punished by the law than alcohol consumption. This seems to be changing, however, at least in Los Angeles. In this city, and I suspect that conditions are similar in most urban areas, marijuana smoking is now conducted quite openly at rock concerts and frequently at other types of gatherings, such as sport events, as well.

The belief that marijuana is a safe or relatively benign drug is becoming more or less entrenched in our society. This is very similar to the attitude that alcohol, since it is legal, is not lethal. In fact you often hear the argument that alcohol is not a drug at all (the liquor industry has conditioned us well). Few people seem to realize the close similarities between

alcohol and the barbiturate drugs. There is an excellent discussion of this in the book *Licit and Illicit Drugs*, published by the Consumer's Union.

As I mentioned earlier, alcohol and marijuana are *not* chemical equivalents, a major difference being the cumulative effect of marijuana, building up in the fatty structures of cells and remaining for considerable periods of time. Marijuana users know that sometimes it takes the beginner several times before the smoking of marijuana produces the desired high (though there are doubtless those who get high because of their expectation that they will—they get high on "atmosphere"). This is because the beginner has no THC residue to build on.

On the other hand, alcohol is a water-soluble food and is metabolized to provide cell energy. It leaves the body rapidly and completely. There is no residue. Although the abuser of alcohol may have a hangover the next day, and in the long run may damage brain and body in various ways, alcohol used in moderation is probably not as harmful as marijuana used in moderation. But since no drug is safe for developing young people, the argument about which drug is "better," or least damaging, is a bit ridiculous.

As Dr. Paton points out, "The price (in health) for (marijuana) overuse is paid in adolescence or in early life; the price for alcohol overuse is paid in later life."

A prevailing myth about marijuana is that it is not physically addictive. Actually, the distinction between a psychologically addictive drug and a physically addictive one is a very fine line, even if such a separation could be logically made. Jones feels that marijuana is chemically (physically) addictive in addition to its obvious psychologically addictive properties. My clinical experience with moderate and heavy marijuana-using adolescents supports Jones's point of view. It appears that since a person can develop tolerance for the drug, progressively more and/or stronger marijuana may be needed to attain the desired high. Any sophisticated young person today has learned the difference between high-quality

marijuana (high THC content), such as Thai Sticks, Maui Wowee, or Columbian Gold, and their relatively low-quality cousins from Mexico or "home grown."

Marijuana users often argue that the drug cannot be addictive, since there are no physical withdrawal symptoms. Actually, such withdrawal symptoms do exist in the form of mild irritability, restlessness, and sleeplessness. The reason the symptoms are mild is that the THC disappears so slowly from the body.

It may be more difficult for a marijuana user to endure the physical withdrawal symptoms than to give up the emotional crutch of marijuana. For pot, as we all know, gives the user feelings of pleasure. This is the whole reason for taking the drug, and it is often an irresistibly compelling reason for continuing its use, especially if the realities of life seem difficult to cope with. The high feelings, Jones feels, are caused by marijuana's *chemical* stimulation of the pleasure centers of the brain, which is why it is impossible to make a real distinction between psychological addiction and physical addiction.

Young people often argue, quite correctly it seems to me, that if marijuana is illegal alcohol should be too. But we tried that, from 1920 to 1933, with Prohibition. The net effect seemed to be not a decrease in the drinking of alcohol but a rise in organized crime dealing in bootleg liquor. And since it appears that people will drink alcohol, take pills, and smoke tobacco or marijuana, in the face of massive amounts of information about their harmful effects, it is unlikely that mere laws will deter them very much. And laws that do not work simply weaken the fabric of all laws.

Let's return now to the promarijuana commentary of Pamela Lloyd concerning the psychological effects of marijuana:

> It is a nearly universal observation among scientific investigators that the *basic personality structure* [italics added] of the subject is of prime importance in determining the subjective nature of the high. . . .

The following alterations of perception are generally reported by subjects and have to some extent been verified by empirical testing:

1. Time periods are perceived as longer than they are.

2. Sounds, particularly music, are felt with unaccustomed immediacy and are understood conceptually, metaphorically, or graphically via translation to fantasy imagery.

3. Visual perception is frequently heightened, while at the same time more subject to misinterpretation . . . pseudo-hallucinations . . . may be fleetingly visualized. Depth perception is altered—objects may appear closer than they really are, but more often appear to be farther away. . . .

4. Most marijuana initiates report a heightened and altered awareness of their bodies, which typically feel incredibly light, as if floating away or apart.

5. And, perhaps at the bottom of all this, *thought patterns themselves are changed by the high. The stream of consciousness seems to swell and float more quickly, bursting traditional barriers (like the one between conscious and subconscious as random ideas surface effortlessly in immediate verbalization).* [italics added]

For the sake of balance, let's make an assumption. Let's say that *all* statements about marijuana, pro and con, are suspect because of possible bias or faulty research design. Let's also assume that all statements have at least a germ of truth in them. With this point of view, we might not be too alarmed at an adult's relatively infrequent use of relatively mild marijuana (or moderate use of alcohol, for that matter), as long as the person is reasonably stable psychologically—that is, not predepressive or prepsychotic. I personally feel that *why* a person uses any drug, even aspirin or tobacco or coffee, is what determines whether the drug is being used appropriately or sensibly or sanely, rather than abused. This is assuming that the use is moderate and the person is functioning adequately, socially or on the job. But I am talking about drug use by adults. In prepuberty and early adolescence, as I have

said, I believe that all drug use should be avoided whenever possible. There is simply too much going on within the young person at this time of life.

We must remember that all of the medical research is not yet in. While much has yet to be learned about the effects of marijuana on the human body, there do appear to be some societies or subsocieties that have long used pot without apparent long-term damage. Yet consider Ms. Lloyd's statement that a primary effect of the marijuana high is that "traditional barriers" (like the one between conscious and subconscious) are broken. This may be fine for an adult who has mind and body more or less "together," as they say. But the bodies, brains, and personalities of our children and early adolescents are still plastic and formative. Their major developmental problem is, almost literally, "getting their heads together." They have a fundamental need to learn to handle their reality confrontations and stresses *creatively* (not by "potting out"). They need to be learning logical, linear thought, and systematic, cause-and-effect-type, problem-solving thinking. Anything that acts to cloud or prevent a young person's reality confrontations does a grave disservice. Whether it is a parent who overprotects, a teacher who awards a too-easy grade, or a drug that prevents the youngster from coming face to face with feelings, limitations, and potentials, all work against healthy development.

I am not saying that it is possible to police our children so that all drugs are ruled out. Not only is it not possible, it is probably not even desirable psychologically or socially, since we would be in danger of overpolicing them. But I do feel that if a society *can* shield its children from the drugs that slow or impair development, it *should* do so. It is highly unfortunate that marijuana is used so widely among young people, just as it would be unfortunate if alcohol and other powerful, mind-altering drugs were widely used at such young ages.

But marijuana is with us now, and with a vengeance. About all we can do is hold the tiger by the tail and urge our

young people to be moderate, while we continue to provide adequate and credible information about all drugs to all members of society. Of course information alone isn't always enough to stop drinkers from drinking or smokers from smoking. And it is not likely that information alone will keep marijuana users from using.

Nevertheless, I will continue to harp on my same old theme. Anything that can interefere with young people's developmental needs should be avoided, prohibited, shunned!

This point of view with my own children, all now in various stages of adolescence or young adulthood, as well as with the young people with whom I counsel professionally, usually has the effect of categorizing me not only as some sort of fossil straight out of a prehistoric era, but rather square-shaped as well. It is a most unpopular, distinctly not "with it" view. Obviously I cannot force young people, or anyone else for that matter, to stop using drugs.

Nonetheless, I have found that as young people learn more about the nature of the changes they are experiencing, and understand more about their identity difficulties, and learn ways to handle stress and plan for the future, many of them tend to decrease their use of drugs (usually marijuana). They also become more selective about timing (for instance, not while studying, only on the weekends) and amount (for example, a few hits instead of a few joints). In short, they move toward a more moderated, recreational use of the drug. Most of the young people with whom I have worked who have moved to this moderate position have functioned more adequately than before in school, on the job, and socially.

As a stress-reducing behavior, pot smoking often reinforces the stress it is supposed to reduce. This self-defeating relationship can be seen in the way potting out interferes with a youngster's development of problem-solving skills, which then increases the need to space out when problems arise.

Marijuana use can be related in the same way to the problem of weight gain. A person's anxiety or self-disgust over being obese might induce the need to feel better and relieve

tension by smoking pot. But pot tends to generate the munchies, in which the smoker has a voracious appetite.

Jennie, a 15-year-old girl some 80 pounds overweight, says:

> I don't know why I can't stop eating or smoking. When you smoke, you eat. It's like being on a diet and going to a candy store. Then, after I've piggied out in the candy store, I can't stand myself so I let a doobie do it for me. It makes me forget what a hog I am. Then, I finish smoking and get the goddam munchies. The whole thing goes round and round.

As I was working on this section of the book, I had a therapy session with a 16-year-old high school boy, Kevin. I would like to quote my process notes for that particular session. Please note that this is *not* a particularly unusual type of conversation between many of my young clients and me. Kevin is fairly representative of many of today's young people.

Process Notes   Kevin X   December 3

Kevin arrived high on pot and immediately told me so. Said that he was about to sit down and study when a friend came over with some "righteous grass" and K. couldn't resist. So, K. smoked out with friend and "shined" studying. This led K. into an expression of an apparently deeply felt worry that he might be an addictive personality type. K. noted that he was getting A and B grades now but he was worried about how he handled stress—there has been alcoholism in the family background. K. feels his mother is "sort of" OK now but still handles stress poorly. K. sees self as handling stress poorly and going on to marijuana too much and too quickly. He places much blame on the school for not watching over things better, though he admits the job is virtually impossible. He also blames fellow students who are into grass heavily, saying that they make it hard to withstand the temptation. So without really

coming to terms with the fact that he, ultimately, makes the decision about whether or not he will engage in pot smoking, K. blames others, even seeing himself as somewhat victimized. Nonetheless, he is now worried about whether he is addicted to pot, and even more worrisome in his eyes is whether or not he has damaged his brain, and become a "burn" (burnout). Ironically, K.'s anxiety, as it goes up, tends to move him back toward the use of pot, which relieves the anxiety and makes him feel good again, in a vicious circle. However, K.'s conversation tonight has actually made *me* feel good, inasmuch as it is the first real hint that he is becoming more aware about the nature of his potential addictive problem, what he is doing to his brain, and so on. Perhaps the first step in coming to terms with oneself is to blame others. At least K. is now beginning to blame someone, which means he is beginning to admit that something is wrong. I am pleased with the session.

The vicious circle relationship between anxiety of various sorts and pot smoking is common. Marijuana provides short-term relief from stress while setting the stage for possibly dire consequences in the long run.

Again and again throughout these pages I talk about stress. It is a factor that must be coped with if a person is to survive in the modern world in a healthy, positive, functioning manner. Norman Cousins, writing in the *Saturday Review*, has stated:

> The more prevalent—and, for all we know, most serious—health problem of our time is stress. The war against microbes has been largely won, but the struggle for equanimity is being lost. It is not just the congestion outside us—a congestion of people, ideas, and issues— but our inner congestion that is hurting us. Our experiences come at us in such profusion and from so many different directions that they are never really sorted out, much less absorbed. The result is clutter and confusion. We gorge the senses and starve the sensitivities.

I am going to close this chapter by quoting two articles, both of which appeared in the *Los Angeles Times*. The article

about drug raids on high schools is, unfortunately, rather common by now in Los Angeles and in other large cities as well. I am including this article as a kind of coda underlining the continuing pot problem with our young.

143 SEIZED IN DRUG RAIDS AT SIX L.A. HIGH SCHOOLS
By Myrna Oliver and Lee Harris

One hundred forty-three youths have been arrested for felony sale of drugs at six Los Angeles high schools in the last four weeks, Police Chief Daryl F. Gates and school district Supt. William Johnston said Friday.

The arrests, made by six undercover narcotics police officers posing as students, included 32 adults, who are campus hangers-on but not students at the high schools and 111 students, eight of them girls, Gates said at the joint press conference. Gates said drug abuse is prevalent and increasing on all school campuses, and that more arrests are planned at other, unnamed schools. He said the six schools had not been singled out for initial arrests because they have any worse drug problem than most other Los Angeles schools.

The six schools where arrests have been made since November 13 represent a broad geographical and ethnic spectrum—Canoga Park and Taft High School in the San Fernando Valley, Wilson High School in East Los Angeles, and Jefferson, Crenshaw and Fremont in South-Central Los Angeles.

Johnston said the school district is "disturbed that it is necessary" but supports the police crackdown on narcotics among students.

The narcotics officers purchased a total of $50,000 worth of marijuana, PCP (also called angel dust), amphetamines, Quaaludes, hashish, cocaine and LSD, a drug popular in the 1960s that Gates said is making a comeback.

The officers found that marijuana is the drug of first choice of students and said its sale and use on campus are commonplace. While marijuana once cost $10 a lid (28 grams), they said, students now buy the highest quality Colombian marijuana, which costs $10 for 4 to 6 grams or "Thai sticks" of 1 to 1.5 grams at $20 each.

High school students also have the money, officers noted, to buy the most expensive drug, cocaine, at $125 a gram.

The youngest student arrested, Gates said, was 14, a ninth-grader from a modest home who had managed to accessorize his bedroom with an expensive water bed, color television and stereo with profits from selling drugs.

One narcotics officer said use of drugs was so common that a physical education class used it as a prize (unknown to the teacher) in a volleyball game. The winners received marijuana, which produces a "high" or "up" feeling, and the losers got Quaaludes a "downer" drug.

Gates and Johnston said the current series of arrests is an attempt to curb increasing sale of drugs on campus and to educate parents to the drug-dealing activities of their children.

Gates attributed recent increases in drug abuse on campus to reduction of penalties for marijuana possession, lack of awareness by parents, and the easy availability of high-quality Colombian marijuana with no feared pollution by paraquat or other contaminants.

The second article, by Harry Nelson the *Times* medical writer, is a bit different. In effect, it says that some of the drug experts who had seemed "soft" on marijuana in previous years were altering their position and now noting the dangers in marijuana use. I have not been consistent in my own stance toward marijuana. Some five to ten years ago I too was easy on marijuana, regarding it as possibly a better drug for society than alcohol. That position gradually changed however, as more and more clinical experience led me to see the devastating effects of the drug on so many youngsters, and as increasing research evidence accumulated negative information. I now regard the near-universal use of marijuana to be one of the worst things that has happened to young people.

Let us end this chapter with Nelson's article:

NEW WARNING FOR POT SMOKERS

Remember the official government reports of a few years ago which said there are no known serious ill effects from the long-term smoking of marijuana?

Viewers of a special NBC News program Sunday at 10 p.m. on Channels 4 and 39 will hear several of the key architects of those reports recant.

Enough evidence has now accumulated to convince them that pot is far from being the innocuous weed that some 4 million American users aged 12 to 17—as well as millions of older users—apparently believe it to be.

"We now know more," Dr. Robert L. DuPont, former director of the National Institute of Drug Abuse, tells correspondent Edwin Newman. "We now realize (the reports) were interpreted by the public as meaning that marijuana is OK. This is a disaster and I feel bad about contributing to that."

The most recent national survey shows that 11% of high school seniors use marijuana daily or near-daily. Three years ago the figure was 6%.

The attitudes about chronic marijuana smoking revealed by four youngsters interviewed by Newman show that their knowledge of the subject is not keeping pace with the scientific evidence.

Street marijuana, according to Newman, is 10 times stronger today than it was four years ago. Coupled with the fact the number of youthful users has nearly doubled in three years, this helps to explain the growing concern about the long-term health consequences of chronic smoking.

Those who continue for years to use this "good" stuff "may be impaired so that they will never function at their best level of effectiveness," Dr. Sidney Cohen, a UCLA psychiatrist and leading marijuana researcher, tells the viewers of "NBC Reports: Reading, Writing and Reefer."

"It is possible," says Cohen, a former federal government drug abuse administrator, "that (these) youngsters will sustain mental impairment that is not reversible."

Skeptics who might believe that Newman has loaded the
dice by his choice of interviewees should take note of
the remarks by R. Keith Stroup, executive director of
the National Organization for Reform of Marijuana
Laws, a group attempting to legalize pot.

He says he is worried about the chronic use of pot by
the young because "there is no such thing as a totally
safe drug and I don't think marijuana will be the first."
Too many young people, he says, have gotten the idea
that because pot is not a killer that is is harmless—or
even a panacea. He warns youngsters about the myth
that it's all right to smoke and then drive a car.

Newman's message is that a way must be found to
inform young people about new evidence which increasingly incriminates marijuana as a health hazard,
especially for the young because they have longer to
live—and, perhaps, to suffer.

I share Newman's hope that a way can be found to inform
young people of the new evidence about marijuana, some of
which is presented in this chapter, though I think the problem
goes beyond marijuana. I believe that as a society we need to
calm down a bit, to begin to see things in a broader perspective and perhaps ultimately develop a sense of ease in our
relationships with each other, including our relationships
with our young. We might then be in a better position to
reduce the use of all of our stress-related drugs. It just may be
that adolescents need much the same thing that the rest of us
do, a general reduction in tension on all fronts.

CHAPTER 14

Your Role as a Parent

Most of us become parents long before we have stopped being children.

Mignon McLaughlin

Since you have read this far into the book, you know that I deeply believe that the more you know about adolescence the better you can help your teenager. Sometimes you have to stand fast and firmly say "no," as with drugs; sometimes you have to step back and let your teenager sink or swim, as with homework or test preparation.

One thing for sure, there is no royal road, no exactly right path. You have to work out what works well within your own family. You can be permissive or you can be authoritarian. But if you are sometimes one and sometimes the other, in unpredictable ways, then you are probably heading for trouble in your relationship with your teenager. However, teenagers tend to throw even the most solid of parents off balance. Your child's unstable nature may cause you to become anxious and unsure of what you are trying to do and why. Your uncertainty is then felt by your teenager. This tends to confuse and even anger the youngster, whose increased confusion can throw you into even more self-doubt, guilt, frustration and anxiety.

Such an emotional mixture tends to be quite explosive. So I would like to touch upon a few concepts which, when combined with the other information that constitutes the bulk of

this book, have been helpful to other parents. But I want to present these comments while once more stating that *there is no way that will "work" with all teenagers and all families.* In fact, in some situations nothing at all will work. Often, no reasonable techniques can be devised to persuade your teenager to follow your wishes.

Your role as a parent is not to coerce your youngster along certain "correct" paths. Such a task is better left to prison wardens or drill sergeants. Perhaps your most important role with your child at any age, and especially with your teenager, is to transmit *values,* a sense of *hope* for the future, and basic concepts having to do with the *meaning* of life.

In these areas as parents we often become unconsciously entwined in our own unresolved attitudes and feelings about who we are and where we are going with our lives. Sometimes we use our children as ego extensions of ourselves. The father who wants his son to become a great athlete may be playing out his own boyhood frustrations, hopes, and dreams. A woman I know had been raised, as she puts it, as a "goody two-shoes." She unconsciously reinforced her daughter's sexual promiscuity, while consciously condemning it.

So, one major part of parenting is to *know thyself.* Look to your own motives if you find yourself pushing hard for a certain prestige school, trying to line up certain "right" acquaintances for your youngster, and so on. Ask yourself if you are really doing these things for the kid or for yourself. Sometimes the answer is a little of both. This may be OK. The main think is that you examine your motives about what you are trying to get your young person to do. You may find that your hidden reason for wanting your child in a particular school or in a specific occupation has little to do with his or best interest.

Another very important part of good parenting with teenagers involves maintaining reasonably positive contact with your youngster. When we are very young we need to meet individuals of the sort philosopher John Locke described

so gracefully as, ". . . civil people who will comply with our ignorance and help us to get out of it." Without good contact with one or more older people it can be very difficult for young people to develop a sense of their place in the world and a concept of hope for the future—their own future, to be exact. It is best, of course, when *you* are the one who can provide this good contact for your youngster, to help in the struggle to develop a feeling for the meaning of life.

Still another aspect of good parenting is to provide your young person, particularly in early adolescence, a benign but definite structure. This means a set of rules or agreements that are reasonable for the youngster's age, peer group status, and living situation; and it also means expectations of "reasonable" behavior at home and at school. The early adolescent, as you will recall, is a fragmented person who is coming apart psychologically and trying to put an identity together. The need for structure in such a situation is obvious. Usually, a parent is the best candidate for providing this structure, although you must realize that this is quite different from the kind of support and regulations you provided when your child was very young. A major task for you now, as your child passes through adolescence, is to judge when and how to gradually give over to the youngster the responsibility for increasing self-discipline and internal structure. By middle and late adolescence, the young person's principal developmental tasks involve learning to set priorities, aim toward goals, and allocate time and energy.

It would be a profound mistake to try to force these responsibilities upon the youngster too early, and unfortunately there are no hard and fast rules here. Some teenagers are much more mature than others. Some teenagers appear to be in danger of falling into an emotional abyss, perhaps involving drugs, perhaps not. And others appear intent on violent or near-violent rebellion toward any and all authority.

Perhaps the most you can expect to achieve is "good enough" parenting, to use Dr. Dan Levinson's phrase. This involves love, judgment, courage, the ability to say no, and,

if necessary, the ability to have your children not like you for a long while. "Good enough" parenting is an art. I am not sure it can be taught. I am not sure it can be learned from a book such as this one. But I am sure that all parents can be helped by thinking about the material in this book and considering how the points might relate to them.

I have said that if you are looking in these pages for a cookbook recipe for handling your teenager, you will be disappointed. No such recipe exists. Anyone who claims to have one is either a charlatan or a bad cook, or both. However, if you can begin to perceive the *adolescent process* as a complex developmental stage, and you can get a feel for the turmoil and turbulence, the confusions and struggles, you will be better prepared to be of assistance to your youngster.

You would probably like to take the emotional pain and pressure off your youngster, if you could. Many parents find that buying this or that won't do it; ranting and raving and setting *more* rules won't do it; ranting and raving and setting *fewer* rules won't do it. If adolescence is confusing for the adolescent, it is also certainly confusing for the parent.

The chapters that follow deal with specific ways of acting and reacting with your teenager. They are intended to help you through confusions you may feel, and help you keep your eye fastened on your ultimate goals for your young person rather than on your own inner turmoil.

In closing this chapter, a brief review of the main ideas may be useful.

1. No one method of parenting "works" always. Sometimes nothing works and all you can do is hold on, allow time to pass, and exercise balance, good judgment, calmness, and as much common sense as you can muster.

2. Teenagers need high consistency from parents to counterbalance their own "coming-unglued" condition. Parents must be, or at least seem to be, "together." Be predictable. Don't send mixed messages. Get your head together about what you believe, what your values are regarding sex, drugs, staying out all night, school work, and so forth, and

don't be afraid to set some expectations for the teenager. You'll be glad you did, and so will your child.

3. Maintain positive contact. This point will be elaborated in Chapter 21.

4. Offer benign but definite structure, especially with early adolescents. This point relates to point 2 above. What is needed are "reasonable" rules and regulations. These can often be worked out with your teenager. Rules and regulations should change as your child grows older. What is right for the 13-year-old may not be appropriate at all for a 16-year-old.

5. Know thyself. Don't be blown out by the argument that someone else's mother (or father) is letting them all sleep over so it's OK. If you aren't comfortable with what is happening, don't be afraid to speak up. Teach your young person to communicate by setting an example of open, positive communication about your feelings, your values, and your concerns. Perhaps your youngster can reassure *you* and change your mind about a particular situation. If so, fine. On the other hand, perhaps the youngster's mind needs to be changed by your thoughts and by your presumably greater and deeper perspective as an adult. If your teenager is relatively young, your wishes will prevail no matter what; with an older teenager, you may or may not want to take the situation as far as a physical confrontation or the threat of asking him or her to leave the home. However, you should want and demand your say about whatever is going on. Without such input your young person is deprived of adult experience and will find it more difficult to mature.

6. If you feel confusion, accept the idea that this is a natural reaction to your teenager's turmoil. Recognize that "good enough" parenting —love, judgment, courage, and common sense—can be very good parenting indeed.

CHAPTER 15

Holding the Emotional Center

The older I got, the smarter my parents became.
Mark Twain

J ust as troubled young people are not sure whether they are fish or fowl, you may not be certain if you are a jail keeper, a helpless observer of trouble about to happen, a custodian of a nice country club who is expected to help out with payments for the car, vacations, pocket money, and the like—or some mixture of all three.

It is most helpful to your emotionally and developmentally unstable young person if you do *not* overly react to teen-age moods, demands, or explosions. *In dealing with instability, try not to become unstable yourself.* It is not helpful to have two unstable bodies orbiting about each other. For people, like planetary bodies, have a tendency to pull each other apart under certain conditions. You must take a position at the "emotional center," allowing the erratic fluctuations of your adolescent to flutter and swing and bounce around you. Because a young person lacks stability and internal structure, you must hold the emotional center and appear stable, from a psychological standpoint, moving on your own track.

On such a course you may well be perceived as old-fashioned, rigid, and "straight." Nevertheless, you offer a central core of meaning. Not that this central core is right for all people. Perhaps it will not be your child's manner of living or ultimate belief system. But as in *Life with Father*, a central

theme of *predictable adult behavior* is being provided. Further, this predictable adult behavior is not moved, swung, or blasted out by the irrational demands or the moodiness of the young person.

If one's identity is not yet well-established, it is helpful to have a touchstone and a model for a reasonably stable identity formation. It is definitely not helpful to have parents who were once thought to be "solid" emotionally shifting about and dancing on the end of the adolescent's own emotional mood strings.

It is also not helpful to a youngster to have parents undergoing life crises of their own. In our present society, this cannot be avoided entirely. For one thing, divorce is at unprecedented levels. In large cities it is now becoming about as likely that one's parents will divorce as that they will not. When marriages break up, children can and often do suffer various forms of psychological damage. Teenagers are sometimes particularly hard hit by the divorce and/or remarriage of their parents. One teenager expresses herself on this matter rather well.

> My folks split. OK, that's bad. But it's cool, too, if that's what they want and what they need. I can see it. They shouldn't have to live together if they are unhappy just for the sake of us [the children in the family]. But I don't know what to do with a swinging father who's gone Gucci and gold on me, smokes grass, and dates chicks close to my age. My mom is all screwed up, too. She is bossing us all around one minute, then cutting out to disco the next. Jesus, who is mothering who around here? She needs more help than I do.

The parent in this case probably does need at least as much help as the teenager. All of their lives are rocketing around in orbit. There is no center of calm, no central value system. And since the teenager does not yet have a mature internal gyroscope that holds on course and steady, most of the stability must come from the adults. So, even if you are going

through your own emotional difficulties and later-age identity problems, you must attempt to muster your energies and hold the emotional center for your child's sake, if not for your own. Actually, doing this will probably help you too.

As a corollary to this concept of holding the emotional center, you need not expect to be popular, or even liked by your adolescent. It is far more important that you have some central core, some basic point of view about life. Remaining clear about your own concepts can be a large problem in a society such as ours, a society fragmented psychologically by various splits and diverse points of view. From a gloomy standpoint, one might perceive our society as "coming apart" in various ways, with no fixed anchoring points. The old reference points of family and extended family, religion, and patriotism are gone or are largely ineffective. But more optimistically, all this coming apart may indicate some good things for the future. Perhaps societies, like adolescents, have their own periods of identity disintegration and reintegration.

Many aspects of our society are changing. As a parent, you have fewer solid guidelines for child raising, since so many of the old ones seem obsolete. Yet this is not a time to weep doomsday tears over the fate of our society, or for the young people growing up in that society.

In fact, there are still sufficient structures to guide parents. For example, if our basic goals for our children involve helping them to feel competent, worthwhile, good about themselves and others, and to behave in civilized and decent ways, then these basic goals surely can be defined.

Let us assume that "civilized behavior," the treating of one another in a humane and decent fashion, is behavior that is learned, rather than simply an innate quality we are born with. In that case, this attitude can be taught. If we value civilized behavior, then we should consider how we may teach it to our children. Our schools could be important in this, but whether they actually offer adequate help in this area is a matter of some debate. With or without the help of

the schools, however, we must try to do what we can to help our children through childhood and adolescence.

A high school senior notes the following:

> No matter what, my parents were really *there* for me when I needed them. They didn't approve of a lot of stuff I was into, especially the drugs. But they hung in there. They didn't understand when I went into my depressions, but they helped me get the right help. They never gave up on me. They talked to me a lot. I even liked when they would challenge some of my far-out ideas. They have been good parents. Good for me. I hope I've been pretty good for them and to them.

In ending this section, let's quickly review some important points.

1. Don't overreact to your teenager. Don't swing with mood swings. Hold steady. Let your child orbit around you, not vice versa.

2. Offer an *emotional center,* a central core of values and meaning. Be predictable. Hold on to your own ideas, though don't be so rigid that you never consider new ideas and concepts.

3. Remember, one of the basic goals of parenting is to develop reasonably civilized young people. They must be able to cope with change in creative ways and not be overwhelmed by the stresses of life. To be able to do these things, they need parents who are steady and who hold out *hope* for them and their future.

4. Provide a model for how to cope with moods, fatigue, joy, sadness, and the general knocks of daily life. How you talk to a policeman or deal with a salesperson is being noticed at some level by your young person. What you do is as important as what you say you do, if not more so.

5. Remember that with a teenager, you are dealing with a prelogical human being. The beginning forms of adult reason and logic are there but they are "as-if" logic systems. You can

be badly fooled (and disappointed) if you assume that your adolescent can readily overcome desires for immediate gratification (a holdover from childhood) and always think through a problem. Even so, keep at it. Keep providing as logical and reasonable a model as you can.

CHAPTER 16

Handling the Anger of the Adolescent

What do I do after he calls me a horse's ass?

A confused parent

The adolescent is a person who is being pulled from childhood's garden of delights into a time of life when parents can no longer solve all problems and the demands of reality are pressing in. Under these circumstances, the young person looks for someone to blame for difficulties and general feelings of self-dissatisfaction. A parent, being close to a teenager physically and emotionally, is an excellent target on which the blame for all problems can be dumped. Of course this is largely displaced or *irrational* anger and is difficult for most of us to deal with in a constructive manner.

I have suggested that whenever your child is acting unreasonably angry or resentful toward you, you should try to remember that this anger or resentment is not necessarily directed at you personally. Often you can defuse explosive situations by depersonalizing them. Of course it is especially difficult to keep your cool in the midst of a family argument when you are being met with stubborn, as-if logic and irrational resentments. If you can keep in mind that you are dealing with an individual who is in a time of great transition and much internal stress, you may be able to de-escalate some of the friction and anger and continue to hold the emotional center.

This is not to say that you and your child may not frequently have many very real disagreements about very real
and legitimate concerns. Such disagreements may well result
in much friction, but hopefully this can be handled well by all
parties concerned. That is, in a logical, rational, courteous
manner.

Keep in mind that even valid disagreements can be aggra-
vated if you overreact to your teenager's anger. Flash points
abound. Arguments can seem to arise out of almost nothing,
about a variety of things, such as your child's manner of
dress, homework poorly done or not done at all, use of the
family car, or the condition of his or her room. The situation
can escalate well beyond the triggering incident. Old wounds
may be reopened as harsh words are spoken. Feelings are hurt
and relationships are damaged. And your heavy reaction to
your adolescent's irrational angers can validate the young
person's feeling that the problems are principally your fault.

It has been said that the secret of dealing with a child or a
teenager is not to be the parent. In my work I often ask troubled parents to imagine that they have volunteered their time
to work under my supervision with a "normally disturbed"
adolescent, not their own, as a paraprofessional counselor. I
request that they imagine the person with whom they are
counseling is very angry toward them, perhaps heaping much
verbal abuse and/or illogic on them, which those of us who
work with adolescents often receive. I also ask that the
parents not take these words or these feelings too personally,
but rather that they *depersonalize* the situation as a therapist
must. The hostility is not entirely meant for the therapist, nor
is it entirely meant for the parents. A large portion of these
feelings express the youngster's inner turmoil, general sense
of instability, and discontent with self.

The words and feelings of William, a 15-year-old involved
in drugs and much family friction, are representative.

> You [meaning me, his psychologist] aren't helping me.
> This is all bullcrap, anyway. It's my parents you ought

to be seeing, not me. No one can make me do what I don't want to do. I'll do what I goddam well please. I'll stay out as late as I want. No one has the right to tell me not to smoke pot in my room. My mother has no right to go in my room. She is screwed up. So are you. So is everything.

I use the phrase, "normally disturbed" adolescent. Parents often question me about this phrase. It probably seems like a contradiction in terms. It will appear more logical when you remember that adolescence is a "disturbed" time, and in the "normal" course of events this happens to all individuals in our society. There are of course many teenagers with psychological disturbances far beyond the normal ranges of adolescence turbulence. These young people require professional psychotherapeutic assistance. It is interesting that on psychological tests, many adolescent profiles resemble those of certain types of adult schizophrenics. The experienced clinician simply makes an age adjustment. What is seriously disturbed for the adult is normal for the adolescent.

Most of us are uncomfortable when others are angry with us, particularly our own children. We are vulnerable to their irrational resentment and demands. We defend ourselves. We are drawn into long explanations of why we want them to meet certain responsibilities and do or do not want them to engage in certain activities or to befriend certain people. But since we are dealing with the "almost" logic of the adolescent, all such discussion is usually a loser's game. It neither persuades nor dissuades the teenager from anything. And any disagreeable decision will make the teenager unhappy. This is OK. Your primary task is to offer logic, structure, perspective, and such wisdom and advice as you can.

This is not easy when you are angry. And for most of us there is a natural tendency to react to anger and illogic with anger and illogic. If feelings are high, reason tends to be low. The best antidote I can offer you is something that one learns in psychotherapeutic training. This is to attempt to get in touch with your feelings but not always to *act* upon them or

react in counterproductive ways. This can be a valuable technique when you feel attacked or challenged by your teenager. Your goals are better served if you can acknowledge your anger to yourself but not let it lead you into an angry response.

If you can hold your emotions at bay in this manner, and further defuse them by depersonalizing your young person's attack, both of you should find it easier to engage in logical and reasonable discussions. For even if they don't change anything such discussions are necessary, as models of reasonably logical thinking. Remember that your rationality does help your young person move toward increasingly rational considerations about cause and effect and the general reality of the world in which someday he or she must function independently. Just don't ever deceive yourself into assuming that your logic gets through entirely or that it will override your child's desires. A child's need for immediate gratification is too high. But each time you are rational and civil, especially when the child is not behaving that way toward you, you are being ultimately helpful.

My basic point is simply that you have to hold firm in the face of sometimes intense anger. This is not a popularity contest. It is an attempt at assisting your young person toward maturity.

Depersonalizing a child's anger is really difficult for most parents. We recall nights when the baby was sick and we worried. We recall anxieties over whether the child had the "right" teacher. We recall loving gifts, vacations, plans, hopes, dreams. We recall these things and so much more, and the anger of that person in front of us—our own child, our flesh and blood, the love of our lives—wilts us and threatens to defeat us.

You must not allow such a defeat. Your defeat and/or your anger cannot be useful to your young person. You must understand the anger, absorb it, stand fast in front of it, never give in to it, and try not to take it too personally.

Let us touch again on the suggestions offered in this chapter.

1. Don't take your teenager's anger too personally. Don't sink to some angry, name-calling level. Be rational and courteous. Discuss, don't launch a physical or verbal attack.

2. Try not to react to anger and illogic with anger and illogic. Anger begets anger. As emotion goes up, reason goes down. You as an adult need to stay calm, no matter what.

3. Remember that you are dealing with a person who is in a time of high transition and high stress, one who is still more child than grown-up, and who does not yet have a fully developed logical system. Keep your expectations geared to these factors. Be kind.

4. It is not your main task in life to make your teenager happy. In fact, usually nothing will make a teenager happy for any great length of time. It is just not a calm, stable, happy time of life for any but the luckiest few. For most, you could give them a new Pontiac Trans-Am and they would find something else to be unhappy about. But while it is not your job to make your teenager happy, it is your task to offer reason, structure, and perspective derived from your life experiences.

5. Never, never, never give in to your young person's temper tantrums, rages, or bad moods. If you do, you demonstrate that constraining authority can be neutralized by anger or moods—highly maladaptive behavior to teach a young person of any age. If you have a raging adolescent before you, if you have just been called a jerk or worse, bail out of the situation with dignity. Simply refuse to discuss the matter until calmness prevails and not before. Indicate clearly that you will not be manipulated by tantrums or moods, but you will be available for a discussion when everyone is under control and reasonable again. Usually, the first time you do this the teenager flips out still further. That's OK. Just hold on to your own emotions and hold steady in the storm. The storm will abate, if you have the courage to hang in there and

insist on a reasonable discussion of whatever is involved. Screaming, breaking things, or running out of the house cause no great harm. More risk is on the other side. That is, if you let yourself be pushed around emotionally, not only will you lose the respect of your child, you will lose respect for yourself as well.

CHAPTER 17

Setting an Example of Dignity and Reason

To behave with dignity is nothing less than to allow others freely to be themselves.

Sol Chaneles

There's a might big difference between good, sound reasons and reasons that sound good.

Burton Hillis

Dr. Albert Bandura, a psychologist at Stanford University, is a leading researcher on *modeling behavior*. Dr. Bandura's work, among other things, underlines how much we human beings learn from merely observing how other human beings handle various situations. If a young person, for example, has a parental model who presents angry, irrational, undignified, and nonsensical behavior, then either the young person must reject the model (perhaps quite sensibly) or follow all or part of it and become a chip off the old block. If a parent's characteristics, under stress, include escalating anger and threats, screaming, or even physical violence, the young person also is likely to adopt those tactics. We learn what we see. We do as others do.

The following are two accounts of parents dealing with what has become, in many families, a highly explosive issue—the use of drugs, specifically marijuana. In both of these families, the parents had decided not to permit marijuana smoking in the home and not allow any of the "pot" paraphernalia, such as bongs (water pipes), roach clips, or

marijuana plants growing under plant lights in the bathroom.

Mrs. Macey's interaction with her 15-year-old son is characteristic of the interactions between this particular mother and her son.

> Mrs. Macey, a housewife in her mid-forties, has four children, the oldest being John, the 15-year-old under discussion. For some years, since approximately the beginning of the boy's puberty, there has been friction between mother and son and, to a lesser extent, between John and his father.
>
> John is an athletic, bright youngster. He plays on the high school football team and maintains an A-B scholastic average. He is handsome and very popular with his peers. However, John is an intense person with high standards for himself. He began using marijuana, he says, in seventh grade, "just because everyone else in school was doing it." John feels that pot helps him relax. He contends that the drug is not harmful, though he admits to being "pretty heavy" into it. John smokes marijuana almost daily, uses Quaaludes something like once every week—and he has even tried Angel Dust (PCP) and LSD. Mrs. Macey has laid down the law to John, stating that he is not to use pot (or other drugs) in the house because she is afraid of the negative influences on the younger children, not to mention the effect on John. Although John agreed to the prohibition on marijuana, he has several times broken the rule and been caught smoking pot in his room, sometimes with friends, sometimes alone.
>
> Following the last time John was "busted" by his mother while smoking pot at home, a terrific argument ensured. As both Mrs. Macey's and John's angry feelings heightened, so did abusive language. Mrs. Macey admits to initiating this phase of their confrontation by calling John a "degenerative doper, an animal, an incorrigible," further stating that she became so angry that she probably used worse terms and even more abusive language on her son.
>
> John, for his part, claims that his mother definitely used more abusive language, while admitting that he was quick to respond. John stated that he called his mother a "bitch," and far more obscene things, and that

he lost his temper to such an extent that be began to choke her. One of the younger children jumped on John's back and, while physically not being able to handle John, at least shocked him back into the reality of what he was doing. John released his mother, with both still screaming at each other. John then left the house in a terrible rage, went to a friend's house and "smoked out" on pot while "doing" some pills as well. Mrs. Macey refused to allow John back into the house. John lived with friends for a while, then moved in with a relative.

John and Mrs. Macey are both losers in the situation. John was angry with himself because of his loss of control and his violent behavior. He still feels his mother's displeasure, while noting that "she has *never* like me, maybe never loved me, since I started with dope and started to do things not her way but my way." Mrs. Macey feels great remorse over the situation, though she still feels that she was right to ban pot from the house. Mrs. Macey and her husband agree that her loss of control was detrimental for John, not to mention the mother-son relationship. They feel that had she been able to handle her own emotions better, the situation possibly could have been resolved more constructively for all concerned, including the younger children who witnessed the fight between mother and son.

In contrast to the above all-out battle between parent and child, Mrs. Roberts, also a woman in her forties, dealt with her teen-age sons, ages 17 and 15, in quite a different manner.

Mrs. Roberts had been divorced some five years before and was not remarried at this point, though she maintained an active social life. The boys' father had remarried, and although he continued a relationship with his sons, the contact grew more minimal and apparently less meaningful as both the father and the two boys developed their separate lives. In general, the mother had to deal with the various problems which arose around two "normal" teenagers.

Deciding that the usual concepts regarding parental control were not feasible in her situation, Mrs. Roberts

evolved a rather unusual approach to the problem of guiding and influencing the behavior of adolescents without falling into severe power struggles. Mrs. Roberts, like Mrs. Macey, held an antidrug position and was especially fearful of marijuana and pills. Unlike Mrs. Macey, however, Mrs. Roberts solidified her position with valid research literature and was firm in her opinion that the drug scene was potentially dangerous for young people. Consequently, Mrs. Roberts took a strong but reasonable position against drug use. She allowed no marijuana or other drugs in her home, throwing out all such material that surfaced there. She pointed out to her sons that their right to privacy did *not* extend to concealing drugs in their room and/or engaging in any behavior which she, as their parent, felt was detrimental or self-destructive to them. And Mrs. Roberts told her sons that if she ever suspected their use of drugs she would engage in "search and destroy" missions in their rooms. Mrs. Roberts' position was that privacy and trust were important, but not as important as trying to prevent her teenagers from becoming involved with drugs. Whether Mrs. Roberts' position was right or wrong is not the issue. The point is, this was a tactic taken by one bold parent to attempt to keep her sons from becoming involved with marijuana or other drugs. Mrs. Roberts' view apparently prevailed. Both sons remained relatively drug free and went on to function well in college.

But one might still ask, how should Mrs. Macey have handled her rebellious and disobedient son?

This is a valid but difficult question. From my viewpoint, escalating the anger was not the answer, and in this case (as in most cases) it produced very negative consequences and no apparent positive results. Mrs. Macey could have held her position against drugs, used her leverage to control John's driving license and his money supply (he did not work and was dependent on an allowance) and attempt to channel him toward more constructive and less drug-involved behavior. And she may have done well to have sought intensive involvement in a family therapy program.

If Mrs. Macey and her husband felt that John had become such a negative example to the younger siblings that he was a danger, they might have considered either a boarding school placement or, lacking funds for this, placement in an institution that works with troubled adolescents. Some parents have had such strong feeling's that they have simply requested that the young person remove himself from their home.

From my viewpoint, I would favor holding the emotional center and not giving in to my anger and disappointment. I would also not support the young person's self-destructive behavior in any way, but I would extend the offer of professional assistance in the form of psychotherapy and/or a substance abuse program. There would be no car, no allowance, no driver's license. I would hope to have the capacity to express my love and continued support on the one hand, while attempting to sever "false" support (cars, allowances, etc.) on the other. This is a tricky game and one which must be played with a fine and steady hand. I strongly recommend professional assistance for any parent caught up in this kind of troubled situation.

An innovative approach used by another parent, Mrs. Arnold, was the use of a "never say no" philosophy on all questions excepting the use of drugs. The simplicity of the concept seems to lend it a very positive power.

> Mrs. Arnold told her teenagers that she would never say no to any of their regular requests, such as staying out on a school night, going to a rock concert in a rough area of the city, or sleeping out on the beach after surfing, *providing* they asked her openly and with full honesty and that she had a chance to discuss fully the pros and cons of their request in terms of its possible consequences. Mrs. Arnold kept her word and her teenagers felt safe in sharing with her their intentions in various matters. Mrs. Arnold allowed them their way if after discussion they still felt that their request was a good one and a reasonable one.

Of course, Mrs. Arnold had great courage and great faith in the judgment and resiliency of her children. Some of their decisions were poor and affected them negatively, such as going to the movies the night before a school test or not fixing the taillights on a car and consequently getting another citation. Nevertheless, the "never say no" technique appeared to offer important, positive intergenerational contact, while at the same time avoiding major power struggles.

Let us summarize the points covered in this chapter.

1. Humans are great observational learners. We learn what we see. We do as others do. Whether we like it or not we are almost constantly setting examples for our children. A major component of "good enough" parenting is to set a sufficient number of reasonably positive examples of how to deal with others and how to handle oneself in a variety of circumstances.

2. A "never say no" philosophy, with some modifications, is an approach that might have merit for you and your teenager. It provides the very important ingredient of positive intergenerational contact and allows a forum for discussion which you might otherwise not get. The never say no approach also avoids major power struggles and sets up a situation in which you can input information and perspective, as well as review potential consequences of the course of action your young person may be contemplating.

One very important point should be noted, however: The never say no technique is definitely *not* recommended for pubertal and early-adolescent children, since they need well-defined guidelines and clearly sent messages regarding yes and no!

CHAPTER 18

Defining Tolerance Limits

What happened to the old guidelines in child-rearing?
Where should I set the limits?

A concerned parent

Parents vary a great deal in the limits they set on their teenager's behavior. Some parents will tolerate the recreational (weekend only) smoking of marijuana or drinking of alcohol, while others cannot bear the thought of their youngsters using any kind of drugs. At what age a teenager is allowed to go out in the evening, how often, and until what time are often major sources of friction within a family. Whether or not the young person should be given an allowance, made to do chores, allowed to drive, are all problems which must be dealt with and resolved in some manner in virtually every household.

Only you can set your tolerance limits and guidance channels for your family. But it is important that you not get locked so tightly into your rules and regulations that you cannot keep revising them as your child grows older. That which is appropriate for your early adolescent probably will become quite obsolete at an older age. Since parents tend to lag behind the rate of change of their young, this differential change rate often produces problems. The young person argues that the rules are now unreasonable, while the more conservative parents tend to hold on to past rules or guidelines that had been working more or less.

One parent who successfully negotiated this dangerous territory with three children recalls how he and his wife had to make constant adjustments and readjustments in their own attitudes, rules, and regulations concerning their teenagers.

> We kept a tight rein on all of them more or less all the way. We did not feel compelled to provide money, though we did pay half for a car when each kid reached 16. However, our position was that the car, like going out on weekends or participating in sports, was a privilege, not a right. If we felt that one of the kids was not coming through and living up to his level of responsibility, then we revoked some privilege. You have to keep changing the rules, though. What the youngest needed was no longer what the oldest needed. We individualized according to the kid's age and the level of responsibility each showed.

It is useful if you realize that, in a sense, you probably do not know your adolescent children very well, just as they do not know themselves very well either. One reason for this is that they are in the process of reforming identity. Another reason is that they change at such a rapid rate that just as you become acquainted with one aspect of identity, another stage in "growing up" has already begun, once more leaving you behind. The acts or attitudes of teenagers surprise so many parents who think they know their young people well, but don't. Maybe they did know the young person well—for a moment or two—before that young person moved on to new thoughts and feelings, not all of which, if any, are shared with parents.

In summary, there are three basic points to be made.

1. You must think about and define your own tolerance limits about what you expect and what you do or do not want from your teenager.

2. You should not wait for your child to define the tolerance limits. Many adolescents will try to push you to the limit, but if you give some thought to how you think things ought to go in your family, you will be surprised at how your

young person falls into line, perhaps with a sense of relief that someone is providing some structure and seems to know what to do.

3. Rules and regulations must change with the age and the responsibility level of your young people.

Approaching middle adolescence, approximately age 16 to 18, more and more of life's responsibilities should be turned over to them. If they continually "blow it" in handling responsibilities, they are signaling that they are not yet ready to assume the burden of maturity. Nonetheless, you must continue to move toward relinquishing the reins or they will never internalize any real sense of responsibility for their own actions. Without the development of the inner sense that they are responsible for what they do or do not do, adulthood cannot be achieved. Without an inner sense of responsibility, a child may continue to blame others for failures, never recognizing the part that the lack of responsibility for one's own actions plays in one's own failures.

CHAPTER 19

Exerting Control

I run the show in my house.

Father of a teen-age boy

I run the show in my house.

The above father's son

In a way, much of the relationship between a parent and a child is a matter of *control*. By this I mean that we oversee and regulate our children, despite the statement, attributed to novelist Philip Wylie, that America is a land ruled by children.

Maybe you have "obeyed" your children when they were young, by catering to their whims, doting on them or spoiling them. Obeying your children can have long-term negative effects. For example, you may find that some of their irrational anger as teenagers is because they can no longer get you to do things their way.

Certainly when your children are young, even if you overly dote on them, you still control many elements of their lives. Parents determine more or less how and where their children spend their time. For example, you may have some influence with their teachers or even a say in who should teach them. You probably arrange their extracurricular activities, allow or do not allow certain TV programs and movies, and perhaps intervene in their peer relationships. When they are very small you select their clothes for them, prepare their food, and control where they play and when.

Young children, knowing nothing else and being relatively small and helpless, allow, tolerate, even encourage your control. It is comforting for children to have good structure and the feeling that someone knows what is needed for them and why.

But as teenagers they are, as the kids say, "in another place." For the adolescent, suddenly grown larger and more mobile and filled with various conflicts, confusions, drives, and other demons, is not so easily controllable.

In the mid-teens you may still be able to control by threatening to deny the privilege of the car or some variation on that theme. This particular threat, it seems to me, should definitely be carried out if you know that there is heavy drug involvement. It is criminal to allow a teenager, who is a novice driver at best, to be on the streets if there is a high likelihood of significant drug use. If your youngster is planning to go out "partying" and you have reason to suspect the presence of alcohol or other drugs, do your best to keep him or her from going. Failing this, try to keep your child out of a car driven by any of the young partygoers. If necessary, arrange to do the driving yourself both ways. If your child has a car and drives *to* a party, you can drive him or her home and promise to retrieve the car the next day. Or else simply let the child sleep over at the partygiver's house, assuming this is acceptable to those parents and you feel that they themselves are not objectionable people.

In addition to controlling your younger teenagers by withholding various privileges, you probably use "grounding," or confinement to the house for a specified number of days, nights or weekends. And no matter what the age of your young persons, you undoubtedly try to control them with your words. For at almost all levels of childhood and adolescence, parents tend to use a lot of words in often vain attempts to manage the behavior of their children. These verbal attempts at influence usually range from reasoned and calm logic to tearful pleading or screaming rage.

Words are not a particularly powerful control factor with

most adolescents, as you may have discovered. Logic rarely works very well with them, though it is better than screaming, yelling, or hitting. In general, reason rarely prevails in human affairs, so why expect too much from this method with your teenager? Obviously, if logic prevailed there would be little need for psychotherapists. If logic ruled you could simply walk into your neighborhood Logician's office and receive a typed out, logical solution for all your problems.

But logic and reason do *not* rule, and certainly not between parents and their teenagers. As your adolescent grows older, you may find that logical breakdowns become more frequent and friction-laden. When push comes to shove between your child's wishes and yours, a power struggle of sometimes ugly and large proportions can loom up quickly. No one can win a power struggle with a loved one. Power struggles are best avoided, if possible, though not at all costs. As I've said, you must hold firm while providing a model for civility and reason. Your teenager may not be so civil or so reasonable. Failing to win the power struggle, which is to say failing to control the situation, the teenager may resort to devious behavior such as lying, half-truths, omissions, or evasions.

In this way you may unavoidably generate a high degree of "adolescent deviousness" in your child. In general, this is no big thing, but it can create a climate of distrust within the family, with much resentment and arguing. Your young person may not seem to understand why he or she is not "trusted," whereas you may consider the child a "total liar."

One young man, Larry, with whom I worked in a counseling relationship for some time, demonstrated extreme deviousness. He had become so devious in his early adolescence that it later hindered relationships with both peers and employers. Larry's deviousness had become, as we say, characterological. It had become part of his identity. This type of happening is, of course, not unusual in our society. We label a person who has a high degree of devious behavior, and no apparent feelings of guilt or remorse about it, as a

sociopath. Some observers on the psychological scene feel that our society may be developing more and more such people, and that perhaps this personality type is rather well qualified for success in the world as we know it. If so, this would be a sad commentary on our culture and our child-raising methods.

In Larry's case, however, he did not feel comfortable with his condition. He recognized that he had, in his own words, become "a habitual liar, cheat, and thief," and he wanted to change. He did, and here is how he brought the change about.

> Larry grew up as a middle child, sandwiched between a "super" older brother and a bright and bewitching younger sister. He was somewhat small for his age as he reached adolescence, was a poor student and not an athlete. At that point in his life, judging by the standards upon which young people tend to be judged (by parents, peers, and themselves), Larry was a loser with little going for him.
>
> By age 13 Larry was a heavy marijuana user. By 14 he had tried it all, including LSD, cocaine, and heroin, though his primary drug continued to be pot.
>
> In addition to Larry's heavy drug involvement, he began to lie chronically in an attempt, he now feels, to make him seem more important than he felt he was. This is not uncommon, of course. But Larry's lying reached the point where he himself could hardly distinguish his distortions of truth from reality. He said, "I would even lie when I didn't need to. It was automatic. Then I would lie to cover one lie with another."
>
> "I stole from my mom and lied. I cheated at school and lied. I was asked a question by a friend and lied. Eventually, everyone kissed me off, including my parents."
>
> In psychotherapy, Larry came to perceive and understand the roots of his chronic deceptions, but he seemed unable to halt or even control the habit. He concluded, "Lies are me. I'm a lie. And I'm screwed."

Finally, however, Larry's one apparently true friend, a girl about a year older than he, told him that she could no longer stand him the way he was. She could not take his deceptions any longer, and until he changed she no longer wanted any part of their friendship. Shocked and frightened, Larry accepted a technique for breaking his chronic lying and cheating behavior. The plan was simple and, for him, effective. He began to keep a daily log of his lying or cheating or anything else he did that he felt was undesirable. He critiqued his own behavior every evening and in his therapy sessions. From a learning theory standpoint, Larry started learning to "discriminate" behaviors, such as lying, which had become automatic or unconscious and constituted a major part of his identity.

As Larry discriminated his undesirable behaviors more keenly, he worked very hard on what he termed "absolute honesty in all things." Further, if he lied, which was still his first tendency in many situations, he tried immediately to correct his lie no matter how difficult or awkward this might be for him.

This program, which Larry and I constructed, worked well. Larry gained respect from his peers. His parents were astounded and delighted. And, having left high school by now, he gained a better-paying job with an excellent future. Of course, best of all was the fact that Larry could finally accept and even like himself. With the assistance of parents, counseling and his own determination, Larry became a person of integrity, with a sense of self-worth. The attitude of the parents was vital here. Not only did they support their son's work in counseling, but they lent great assistance by letting him know that they believed he could and would solve his own problems and become his own person.

Here are some summarizing points and further suggestions concerning control.

1. Who controls whom, in what ways and for what purposes, is often a hidden agenda in families. As a parent you obviously exercise various kinds of control over your children, even the older ones who may have moved off to

college or out into their own apartments. This parental control is direct and total when a child is young, but becomes indirect and partial with older teenagers.

In any case, as with structure, the types of influence or control you use must change with the age and the personality makeup of your young person if it is to be effective. Most parents tend to use some form of punishment in order to control their children. Actually, it can be demonstrated that for most human interactions, perhaps especially among family members, punishment is rather ineffective and inefficient and has a number of negative side effects.

I suggest that punishment be kept to a minimum in raising children. Certainly it is necessary at times for a young person to suffer some consequences for unacceptable behavior, consequences such as grounding, loss of driving privileges, and the like. But many parents don't use this technique as effectively as they might. For example, parents often decide on the punishment *after* the fact. When the young person comes home after curfew some punishment such as grounding for the next week or so may then be imposed. This punishment may not work, and in any case there is a more effective way of doing it, which is to spell out the contingencies in advance. "If-then" statements can be a strong tool in doing this. This method not only tends to help keep your youngster's behavior within certain limits, it also teaches that behavior does, in fact, have consequences.

The if-then method is quite simple and straightforward. For example, you might say to your teenager, "*If* you are later than ten minutes or so past your curfew time tonight, *then* no car for you next weekend." You have now hit the ball into the other court. If the youngster doesn't come through on this reasonable expectation, then the use of the car on the following weekend is forfeited. Kids may initially fail to see that it is not you who are doing the punishing, but they will gradually come to perceive that it is their own behavior that creates the problem, not some arbitrary whim of yours. This is a valuable lesson, indeed. There is no more important

lesson to learn than that we are each responsible for our own actions and that we each enjoy or suffer the consequences of them.

2. Power struggles between you and your teenager are best avoided whenever possible. The use of if-then contingency statements can be helpful, provided that your child is at an age where you still have the control to impose consequences. This does not mean that the youngster is going to be happy about your holding to the consequences (and you *must* hold to them once you have stated them—say what you mean and mean what you say). There will be arguments or even tantrums. Obviously, you do not give in to such behavior and you do not get involved in an argument. The contingencies were clearly stated, and now you insist upon compliance. You can sometimes even align yourself with the child and actually feel genuinely sorry that unacceptable behavior has caused loss of the use of the car, grounding, or whatever. The only thing you must not do is break off the contingency and give in. An exception would be if you found that, for some reason, you had been wrong and/or there had been truly mitigating circumstances. You may not have communicated your intent clearly, for example, or the youngster may have had a flat tire.

In good enough parenting, consistency is a great virtue. But you have to use common sense and know when to be a bit flexible too. As Ralph Waldo Emerson said, "A foolish consistency is the hobgoblin of little minds."

3. In the example of Larry, the control methods used by his parents eventually resulted in his becoming so devious that he lied to himself. Although this is a somewhat extreme example, deviousness and distortions between parent and young person do often exist. But they can be minimized if good, positive, open lines of communication can be maintained. It is primarily your job to maintain these communication channels with your teenagers, since they cannot really be expected to have either the skills or the motivation to do so.

Sometimes parents are confronted with an absolutely rebellious and uncontrollable teenager. At that moment there may be nothing you can do and, as when therapists are dealing with potentially dangerous patients, it may be best to attempt to neutralize the situation. If you are in an argument, bail out by saying that both of you (your teenager and you) are too emotional to discuss anything any further right now. If the child is walking out of the house and going somewhere without permission, keep cool but state that there will be consequences for this behavior. This gives you some time to think and to discuss the matter further with spouse, friends, or a counselor. If the youngster is becoming violent do not react with violence. Violence only breeds more violence, usually making matters worse. If your child is on drugs and becoming violent, be especially careful. You probably are not dealing with the child you know at all and you can't tell what is happening in a chemically clouded mind. Try to keep calm and try to talk the child down. This technique will be explained more fully below. But, if you are too frightened or upset, don't try this talking down technique yourself. Get some help. Call a hot line service or a professional therapist. Don't be ashamed. Get help. In the extreme, call the police.

For an individual at the end of his or her emotional rope and/or wired on drugs (often some type of speed) the technique of "talking the person down" is often useful. The essence of the technique is that you just sit and keep talking with the person in a kind, soft, nonjudgmental and non-attacking way. Do not be condescending. Your tone should be that of one in a friendly conversation. You are interested in the individual's anger, sadnesses, or whatever, but not playing into them or reinforcing them. You listen and you ask appropriate questions. You keep the person talking, often for hours. You will be able to see that the person is "coming down" by his or her behavior. Gradually, if things are going right, the person will become calmer and somewhat more rational. Finally, after thousands of words, the individual

tends to become fatigued and will sometimes rest or even go to sleep. You may be hoarse for a day or so, but you will have blunted the trouble.

Nonetheless, in any of the above scenarios (and many others could be added), the signs are clear that you and your teenager need professional assistance. As soon as possible, contact a psychotherapist who deals with adolescents. Names of such therapists can be obtained from your county or state psychological, psychiatric, or social work organizations. These organizations are listed in the phone book.

CHAPTER 20

Coping with the Teenager's Need for Immediacy

But I don't want to wait until my grades improve. I want my driver's license *now*.

A sixteen-year-old

Like the younger child, the adolescent seems to have a strong tendency toward the "I want what I want when I want it syndrome." Perhaps all of us tend to judge the merits of an activity by what it offers right now. But this seems especially true for the teenager, who, much more than the adult, lives in the present. Although the young person may think about the future, that thinking is probably more akin to worry, and includes only the vaguest notion of the preparations needed for what lies ahead.

We all have anxieties about the future. We are told there will or will not be sufficient food and energy. We are uncertain of how to invest our money. We worry whether our retirement income will suffice when we can no longer work. We are afraid of lawsuits in our litigious society. We are afraid of not having a strong army. We are concerned about spending too much on welfare. We feel guilty about not doing enough for poor people. There is a seemingly unending list of worries and doubts about our individual futures, the future of the country, and even the future of the human race.

Faced with this great jungle of worries in the adult sector, it is no wonder that many adolescents tend to withdraw into drugs or even regress emotionally.

Many teens drop out of the rat race before they are ever in

it. Others hang in their but have deep feelings of inadequacy about coping with an ever-changing world.

As adults, we often talk about preparing our children for later life. By this we usually mean assisting them to earn good grades in school and stay out of trouble. Our ultimate aim for them is to see that they are prepared, through formal education or vocational training, for some kind of job or career that will give them, hopefully, both financial and emotional rewards.

For the most part, such ideas appear remote and vague to adolescents themselves. In fact, the idea of preparing for their unknown future may be rather disquieting. For many teenagers, the future is a dark forest filled with strange and perhaps fearful beings and events, a place in which they are to be tested and perhaps found wanting.

Given this point of view, it's not surprising that many young people want to put off for as long as possible any serious preparation for their future. They prefer to immerse themselves in the new and hold on to the comforting structure of the present. The gratifications of *now*, such as driving around with friends, playing electronic games, going to parties, and having a nice place to eat and sleep without having to pay for it, all exert a stronger pull than worries of *then*, with all of tomorrow's concerns, responsibilities, and problems to be handled and hassled.

A highly literate teenager expresses this idea well.

Time is of the essence. I like to believe that one should live for now . . . I used to be obsessed with the fear of growing old . . . I never want to grow old and sit and say I should have done this or that, I wrote this poem about growing old . . .

Hurry, hurry
Youth's slipping fast
Come over
Before the candle
Burns too low
And the wax cools

I guess everyone has these fears, but with me the fears started growing at age 14 or so. And, what's really strange is that I've blocked out a lot of my childhood hours. Significant? I don't know.

The teenager's frequent need for immediate gratification, or *immediacy*, seems to be a leftover childhood tendency simply not yet outgrown. It may also be, partially, a psychological defense mechanism, developed largely to ward off the anxiety buildup which ensues when the adolescent must face the need to function in the world as an adult. We can hardly blame our children for wanting to ward off this inevitability. And we ourselves often would protect ourselves from the harsher realities of adulthood if we could. For is there not some Peter Pan in all of us?

But how can you as a parent help?

There is not too much you can do about your children's leftover tendency to require immediate gratification, except to continue not shielding them from reality confrontations. They will eventually grow out of this tendency unless you help them perpetuate it. If you fill out the college admission forms or fill out employment papers, provide cars, hand out spending money, vacations, and the like, on a virtual noncontingent basis, you are *not* helping them learn to struggle their own struggles and hassle their own hassles. Some parents who over-help are unconsciously undermining the development of competency in their own children. They may even need their young to be dependent on them because it gives such parents a sense of meaning and purpose.

Richard's case is representative of overgratified, "immediate," young people.

Richard is the oldest son of a very wealthy and powerful man. Richard has been given the "best of everything" for all of his life, including a new Chevy Camaro Z/28 on his 16th birthday. He has never had to work at a job. In school, any subjects which were difficult were dropped by parental intervention.

Most people would probably like Richard as an individual, and most would like his father. The relationship between father and son is, by most standards, fairly good. Richard is obviously very spoiled and rather materialistic and pouty. Father likes to play Big Daddy and shows off a bit with all this giving. Nonetheless, both father and son are "nice guys." However, at age 24 Richard is still a lost, dependent, floundering individual. He is still drifting from one major to another in one college after another. These colleges are all academically low-powered, because Richard cannot muster the self-discipline to handle any significant degree of academic work.

Richard has become increasingly resentful of his father. We tend to resent those upon whom we are dependent. As Richard has matured psychologically, he perceives his father as having impaired his development, as having given too much too easily, and as having undermined Richard's feelings of self-worth and self-confidence by never allowing or *making it necessary* that he do much struggling, thinking, or problem solving on his own.

As Richard has increasingly realized the nature of what has been done to him throughout his life, and this by a well-meaning and doting father, he has become increasingly independent and courageous in moving away from father's protective wing and into situations in which he is on his own. This includes not working for any of his father's various companies. At 24, Richard is now working in a T-shirt store as a salesclerk. Nonetheless, he is satisfied that he is moving in the right direction, toward independence, though he is still extremely ambivalent over his manner of upbringing and whether or not he can succeed on his own.

Using the word "spoiled" to describe a young person is interesting. If food, for example, is spoiled it is understood that it has been mishandled in some manner and is no longer useful. The same goes for various other aspects of our lives—such as a spoiled paint job or a "spoiler," which in sports is an individual or team that ruins another's record of success. Sometimes parents may need to deny themselves the

immediate pleasures of "doing for" and possibly spoiling the young person. A significant parental gift is to step back and allow our young to learn to do for themselves!

What about the other aspect of your young people's struggle, the psychological defense mechanism that helps them avoid facing the frightening future? How can you help them in this struggle? You can do the same thing you might do with other people overly concerned about success versus failure, which is to help them develop feelings of *competency at their current levels of life*. This means helping the young persons strengthen their perceptions of their abilities to cope with the ups and downs of life and to function in an integrated and positive manner psychologically and intellectually.

The essential key to your teenager's developing this perception of being self-worthy is fairly continuous and consistent contact with one or more adults who are "kind guides" (that important intergenerational contact). Teenagers need guides who can accept the deep insecurities that are a part of life—not just their lives, but all life—yet who are not overwhelmed by doubts and uncertainties. These guides must offer them the belief that they too can succeed in handling the complexities of the world. Your adolescents need, as we all do, someone who believes in their skills and competencies or at least in their ability to develop them ultimately, and who has *hope* for their future.

As your child's parent, you may be in the best position to be this guide. If for some reason you cannot fill the role, perhaps you know some other person whose opinion your child respects and who cares—maybe a grandparent, a teacher, or an older sibling. Enlist that person as a guide, to keep contact with the child, express concern for his or her well-being, and transmit the underlying feeling that the child will make it.

Consider the major points covered in this chapter:

1. We parents often send mixed messages. We tend to fear-condition our young. How many of us have, one way or another, "told" our children that if they weren't successes in

school they would be failures in life? And they get the same message in school: "If you don't get good grades you can't do well here; if you can't do well in school, you will not get a good job." And so on and so on.

Parents often talk about how hard the world is and how difficult things are. No wonder many young people perceive the adult work as a major downer, a very depressing place. Offer the young some hope! Send the message that life is complicated and sometimes quite difficult, but nothing that can't be handled. Your teenager is just getting a personality together and needs some feeling from parents, that he or she will not only get it together, but also pick it up and be a terrific success!

2. Don't try to shield your teenagers from reality confrontations. They must learn to experience the consequences of their own actions or lack of action. This does not mean you ought to hold back on sympathy and/or advice if they are really down, confused, and feeling blue. But don't allow them to feel that in some way *you* should have solved problems for them or that the problems are someone else's fault, not theirs. And I am talking, of course, about a situation in which your teenager has blown it. We all know that some problems really are someone else's fault, and some are no one's fault at all.

3. Try to reinforce your teenager's feelings of competency and confidence. Teenagers are shaky people, as we know. It is important to them that you believe in their capacity.

4. Try to envision yourself as a "kind guide" for your teenagers. We parents are not here just to pound our values and our way of doing things into their little heads. Other, perhaps even more important, functions are to teach, advise, suggest, confront, support, and serve as models for reasonable, decent behavior.

CHAPTER 21

Spending Quality Time Together

He who wastes time, injures eternity.
Henry David Thoreau

While you may not be injuring eternity by wasting or not spending quality time with your youngsters, you may not be building good relationships with them or offering them sufficient chances for positive intergenerational contact.

When your children are young, there is usually little problem about spending time with them. If you are so inclined, almost any activity will do for the young child, who is usually glad to have your company and delighted with your attention. Incidentally, many parents delude themselves into believing that they are "spending time" with their children when they go places as a family, such as to the beach, on vacation, or to the movies. Such outings are important, but largely involve time spent in a *group*, with various group rivalries and frictions. This is not the same as individualized time. But spending individualized time with a child is fairly simple. You can take a walk, go for a bike ride, go for ice cream and, in general, talk and have fun together.

 With adolescent children, however, there is a difference. They tend to be more involved with peers and peer-related activities. Teenagers may even feel it is awkward to spend time alone with parents. Even if they are willing, you may be at a loss over where to go or what to do with them.

There is no one way to provide individualized quality time. The best way depends upon what you and your

teenager have in common and what works out most comfortably from both your standpoints. You should take care not to turn such time into "sessions" involving probes about activities or criticisms of behavior. When the criticism starts it is the kiss of death. Also, time spent with your teenager need not be an all-day marathon of togetherness. A little while will suffice if the time is spent pleasantly and cordially.

Those who break bread together, as good salesmen know, tend to develop positive feelings toward each other. Thus, I often suggest that *one* of the parents should have lunch or dinner with their teenager once a week or every two weeks. Both parents can share in this activity, by working out some sort of alternating arrangement. To derive maximum gain from a "time spent" standpoint, the following guidelines seem important:

1. Try to choose a sit-down restaurant, rather than a fast-food outlet. Thus, you have to sit down, order, and wait. While waiting, there are generally enough other people and other things going on so that you and your teenager do not have to maintain heavy eye contact or strain to fill conversational gaps. Also, it is more difficult to get into an argument or a shouting match in a restaurant than it is at home, since the environment imposes restraints and civilized behavior.

2. Don't lecture. Keep the conversation neutral. This is not the time to chastise or argue with your teenager. Enjoy the food and each other's company. Learn how to converse *with* as opposed to talk *to* your young person.

3. As the adult you should bear in mind that you are serving as a model of how to conduct oneself, how to carry on a conversation, how to explore the world of ideas. The implication is that soon, if not at once, your adolescent will be entering the adult world and be on equal status in places such as restaurants, and in activities such as social or work gatherings of all age groups, including jobs.

4. Despite these meetings, you should not confuse your teenager by trying to become a friend instead of a parent. The meals and the conversation are, hopefully, friendly. But the role relationship of parent and child must not be blurred.

Your teenager needs a parent, not some new buddy. These meetings are to facilitate good intergenerational contact. You could even share with your teenager *some* of your business or other concerns, as well as something about who you are as a person from a value standpoint. But when you share such concerns, do not transmit them with any sense of defeat or despair. Remember that you are talking to an immature and basically insecure person. You should try to project the attitude that problems can be solved, puzzles can be unraveled, and the adult world also has its many joys.

5. Don't go to an expensive restaurant unless you want to communicate to your teenager that money really just doesn't matter to you. You can teach valuable lessons about good food at fair prices in nice surroundings, and extend such "lessons" to many other things in life.

6. Again, don't lecture.

7. There are activities other than having lunch or dinner together that you might do with your teenager, depending on your relationship and your mutual interests. Going to a movie or a sports event together, followed by having something to eat and a brief time for talking, can be quality time. And important time can be spent with your teenager if you are lucky enough to share interests in projects such as constructing something together, or motorcycle riding, or cooking, or scuba diving, especially if your youngster is building up confidence and competence in one or more of these activities. However, this kind of togetherness takes some sensitivity on your part in order to avoid using the occasion to show off your own skill rather than letting it be a shared event. You also need to be sensitive to whether your teenager really wants to engage in these activities with you. And don't be too disappointed if you realize that he or she would rather do them alone or with a friend.

No matter what activity you pursue with your youngster, the same guidelines apply about remaining a model for getting along in the world, not being critical, demonstrating some confidence in your child and the world in general, and enjoying your teenager's company.

CHAPTER 22

Psychotherapy with Adolescents

I like my sessions with my shrink. We talk about a lot of stuff. It's not me just getting my feelings out, though that helps. She teaches me a lot, too. Like relying on the withdrawal method during sex isn't too great and how different drugs effect you in different ways. My shrink is a special kind of tutor.
Teen-age girl talking about her psychotherapy sessions

. . . formal psychotherapy [is] a specific personal individualized intervention [focusing on] the patient's sensitivities to life situations and his personal reactions to life experiences; on gaining insight into these susceptibilities in an effort to strengthen his ability to deal with himself and his reactions; and on gaining mastery of his life situation.
Philip May in Handbook of Psychotherapy and Behavior Change

This chapter is not intended to serve as a consumer's guide to psychotherapy. Instead, it offers you a sampling of the types of worries, difficulties, confusions, and sadnesses that adolescents bring into my office and the offices of other counselors of the young. The intent is also to provide some flavor of how at least one therapist, the author, perceives the "doing" of psychotherapy with this age group. I hope that the illustration and discussion of some of the more serious problems of teenagers will help make the general developmental problems of adolescence more understandable.

With the early-adolescent patient, I tend to do a large amount of counseling work with the parents as well as the young person. Sometimes it is useful to meet with the entire family, or the teenager and the parents. In general, I favor individual sessions for the young person, with separate parent conferences. In most instances, once-per-week appointments for the young person suffice, with parent conferences on a less frequent basis.

Sessions for the adolescent need to be on a consistent basis. I think of them as a form of tutoring. In addition to working on the young person's particular difficulty—phobia, depression, anorexic reaction, drug abuse, sexual dysfunction, homosexuality, or general anxiety state—the teenager needs also to come to a better understanding of the various aspects of the adolescent phase of development.

The therapist must also offer strong support to the parents. It makes little sense to me to work exclusively with the young person, especially an early- or middle-adolescent who is not yet an autonomous person. The parents are a necessary part of the scene. And parents also need a great deal of assistance in understanding both the general process of adolescence as well as what, if anything, they can do to assist in resolving their child's problems. The therapist needs to help parents hold the emotional center, not waffle too much on basic issues or principles, not permit themselves to be overcome by self-doubts, remain consistent, and work toward the development of the appropriate home and/or school reinforcement programs which are a vital part of the therapeutic work with many young people.

Reinforcement means strengthening some behavior or set of behaviors, for example, responsibility or truthfulness. Often they are best strengthened through the use of the contingency statement, which we have discussed. "If you do not study, then you lose the privilege of television." Or on a more positive note, "If you get your chores done, then you may ride the trail bike up in the hills." There are some excellent books that spell out these very useful reinforcement and

contingency concepts in more detail. Among the best is Gerald Patterson's *Families* (Research Press).

In this section I have selected several cases that are more or less typical of the types of problems that the therapist specializing with adolescents might encounter in a private practice or outpatient clinic. Names and details have been changed, of course. Some of the young people I work with have far more serious problems than those illustrated here, problems such as paranoid schizophrenia, anorexia nervosa, and autism. But these more severe psychological problems, while important and interesting, are not relevant to our main focus on typical adolescent difficulties and the general understanding of the adolescent process.

CELESTE (15)

Celeste developed a phobia to school and demonstrated an extreme general withdrawal reaction during the eighth grade after experiencing a *grand mal* seizure at school. Not only was she embarrassed when she regained consciousness, but her anxiety built up to an extremely high level when school officials dallied and delayed for some time before notifying her parents and physician. For a year and a half following the episode, Celeste did not return to school. She spent the remainder of the eighth grade and all of the ninth grade in a home-teaching program in which the school district provided lessons and examinations by telephone. Celeste never left her house except for brief excursions with her parents.

During the latter part of the ninth grade, Celeste was referred to me by her psychotherapist because the therapist felt she was not effectively assisting Celeste with her problems. This was a highly honest and ethical move on the part of the therapist. It seems to me that all therapists should consider carefully their degree of effectiveness (or ineffectiveness) with each client. An important theme of current research in psychotherapy is in the area of match-up between client and therapist, which is considered a major variable in success or failure of the therapeutic enterprise.

I judged Celeste to be shy in the new situation, her shyness compounded by the switch from female to male therapist. Incidentally, a good case can be made for having a therapist of the same sex, especially with an early adolescent client, and I often refer prepubertal and pubescent girls to a female associate. However, in Celeste's case, there were some very good reasons, involving family background and her relationship with her father, which indicated that a male therapist might be useful.

Celeste was ambivalent about "getting better." Getting better in her case meant leaving the protective womb created around her by family and, inadvertently, by the school's home-tutoring system. I decided to take a therapeutic risk early in the game. In our third session I discussed Celeste's attitude with her. I pointed out the manner in which she was controlling her situation, as well as the probable ambivalence that she was feeling about me specifically and about changing her behavior generally.

I then suggested that Celeste return to therapy with her previous therapist or let me refer her to someone else with whom she might relate well. I asked her permission to talk to her mother about this, following which the three of us discussed the situation. Before the session ended, I told Celeste that counseling of this sort involved our mutual participation. I said that I was not in any hurry or trying to push her. I told her that our goal was not necessarily to return her to school, but rather to help her feel confident about herself in any situation. In closing, I told her that if she should keep her next appointment, I would consider that to be her statement that she wanted to overcome her problems and was willing to work with me at doing so. In essence, she must commit herself to sincerely working, or else leave.

Later I telephoned Celeste's mother (who was obviously upset and frightened by my confrontation, not wanting to lose a second therapist) and requested that she not urge Celeste to continue with me, but allow the youngster to make her own decision. I explained that it seemed clear to me that

Celeste's behavior was controlling too much of everyone else's behavior, especially the parents'. I felt it vitally necessary that the parents not reinforce Celeste's manipulations or her anxieties by pleading with her to keep her appointments with me or to return to school. The mother was able to follow this suggestion. Celeste showed up for her next appointment a week later, and began to improve.

Over the next month or so, on once-per-week visits, Celeste and I worked on two major themes simultaneously. One theme, almost a hidden agenda in the sense that neither of us spoke of it openly, was our relationship with each other. Celeste had an extremely distant relationship with her father, had no brothers, and had never had a boy friend. As became apparent, many of her fears revolved around her insecurities with people in general, but it was with males that her fears were greatest. The slow development of friendship, trust, and warmth between Celeste and me became a large part of her therapy.

The other major theme during this aspect of Celeste's therapy was her high need to control her life in all its aspects. This need for control seemed closely linked to her deep fear of loss of control, as represented by a seizure, during which she might fall, become incontinent, and in her words, "look funny."

Such feelings certainly were understandable. And they were even more heightened by her typical adolescent feelings of acute self-consciousness, both in her social skills and in her appearance.

Gradually, as our rapport warmed and Celeste's trust in me developed, I began to introduce more and more the subject that I felt she actually feared. I moved the conversation often to her social life (at this point, she virtually had none), or at least to how she envisioned it as developing over the next few years. At first the introduction of such material heightened her anxiety level considerably and also depressed her.

I continued to point out Celeste's anxiety to her, explaining that it was only natural for her to be frightened about this

aspect of her life and that nearly all other teenagers were too. I told her that she must allow me to continue dealing with this subject as well as others that might discomfort her. With good courage, Celeste increasingly grappled with her anxieties about socialization with peers. We began to talk at length about how girls related to girls, girls to boys, boys to girls, and children to parents. This technique is called informal desensitization. It is a very powerful tool for anyone attempting to help another overcome deep-seated fears.

As this general conversational path continued, Celeste and I moved into discussion of her feelings of differentness, in which we had to separate carefully how much was due to her general adolescent phase (it was news to Celeste, for example, that almost everyone else felt different too) and how much was a function of her epileptic condition. Increasingly Celeste was able to discuss her fears of having a seizure while out with peers at a party or movie and being terribly embarrassed. The more we talked, the less she seemed to be afraid. In our heads, and with our words, we played out countless scenarios involving Celeste and peers—what might happen and how she might react. Eventually she brought up the fact that she felt different also because her parents were "too old." Her parents were, in fact, in their sixties, which was older than the parents of most of her friends. Celeste felt also that her parents could never help her because they could not understand her. She manifested all the irrational anger that teenagers so often feel toward parents. My rapport with her was now sufficient to sustain hard confrontations. I met her parent-anger statements head-on by (1) interpreting them as displaced anger and a general attempt to lay blame for her own feelings of inadequacy at someone else's feet and (2) pointing out to her, as I do to all teenagers, that at some point one must take responsibility for one's life *no matter what* parents did or did not do for, or to, one in earlier years.

By this time, we had moved into the summer between ninth and tenth grades. Celeste's seizures were under excellent control and only mild amounts of medication were needed to

maintain her seizure-free status. Celeste was, however, already beating the drum for continuation of her home-tutoring program, citing all sorts of reasons why this would be better for her. I continued to employ the informal desensitization approach, focusing heavily on peer relations. My main point to Celeste was that school was not only important for academic learning, but it was a vital place for social learning. I told her that I hoped she would not elect to continue to miss the fun, frustrations, joys, and tensions of an active school social life. At the same time, I continued to hold out to her a future hope and expectation that she could and would function well in the high school milieu.

In midsummer, Celeste opened one of our sessions as follows:

"OK. Find a school for me."

(You have decided on a private school?)

"I was going to go to Uni [University High School], but everyone says it's too big, too impersonal."

(Who is "everyone"?)

"Me. Whomever. I don't know. It doesn't matter. I think I'd do better in a small school. Besides, that's your theory too, isn't it? Smaller schools for teenagers so they can get to know the teachers better and all."

(Yes, that is my theory too. OK, I'll get to work on it.)

"Just make sure the kids aren't weird. And that I can do the work."

(I'll give you the names of several good schools to go and take a look at. You can make sure for yourself that the kids aren't weird. Maybe you can check them out before summer school is over.)

"What if I get sick there? What will happen? Are you going to tell them about me, that I might get sick?"

(Yes, of course. I'll make sure that the people in the office know just how to handle things if you get sick. What happened before won't happen again. But even if it did, you are different now. You would know how to handle the situation yourself much better than that other time.)

"I hope that I can handle the work OK. Home tutoring for so long . . . maybe it's screwed me up as a student. Do you think I'll have to take notes? I don't know how to take notes. It scares me."

(Maybe we can get you into the second session of summer school.)

"Yeah. Try that. No. I know what you are going to say. That it is up to *me* to try it, to figure it all out. What would you do if I was your daughter? Did you really not help your daughter get into college? Do you really think I can do it?

(I really do think you can do it.)

You may detect the transference aspects in the above exchange, with Celeste partially wondering what it would be like if I were her father. Her allusion to my daughter was also because I had discussed my attitude toward my children more than once, including the fact that I felt that if my daughter was not intelligent and mature enough to figure out how to graduate from high school and get herself into college, then she wasn't ready for college yet. And in any case, I had no intention of helping her by filling out applications or nagging her. Celeste knew that I felt my daughter's life was hers to develop or not develop as she saw fit, just as was Celeste's.

I should mention that almost all the teenagers I work with are highly interested in my attitude toward my own five children (two are stepchildren). I do not believe that this interest is all a part of some transference phenomenon involv-

ing me as father figure, though this is surely one aspect. I feel that most of the young people are looking for perspective, comparing one parent's behavior with that of another, and are often amazed at my relatively "hard" approach with my own teenagers—"hard" meaning laissez-faire about such matters as whether the youngster gets himself over to take the college entrance exam or not, or gets to the Department of Motor Vehicles for a driving license exam or not, and so on.

I believe older adolescents must learn to take responsibility for their own behavior, and that they will not get an education, a job, or anything else on my account but on theirs. I am not easy either on matters of common courtesy within the home. I insist on reasonably civilized behavior on the part of all who live under my roof. I am not easy on drugs, absolutely banning possession or use in my home. My older children, now college age and living away, must decide for themselves about the various drugs of the culture. But in my home I still set the structure. That said, let us return to Celeste.

Celeste attended a small private school during the second summer session. She manifested great anxiety at first but, gradually and with increasing ease, was able to separate from her mother who drove her to school in the morning. Celeste then enrolled in the same school for the regular tenth grade session. At this writing, midway through the year, Celeste attends school regularly, is seizure-free, and is doing well academically. As might be expected, however, after missing over a year of any significant interaction with peers she is still shy, insecure, and socially awkward. Currently, Celeste and I spend a good deal of time discussing how to overcome her social skill deficit and concomitant feelings of inferiority. She has accepted my suggestion that she participate in a teen-age rap group run by one of my associates. With reasonable luck, Celeste will make it socially and academically.

ALEX (14)

Until about age 12 or 13, Alex had been a reasonably good student and no particular trouble at home or elsewhere. Then, his parent said, "He just went bananas." His grades

went down, he became increasingly disorganized in all aspects of his life, and he varied in mood from general surliness to intense hostility toward his mother and father and older sister.

Alex's parents were shocked and surprised at his behavior. Initially, they met his demands and hostilities with inconsistencies, varying from get-tough policies on which they found they could not follow through, to permissive policies which made them feel uncomfortable and led to no perceptible diminution in Alex's surliness and moods anyway.

Finally, the parents discussed the problem with the director of their son's school, who referred the family to me. As in most cases, prior to initiating a program of psychotherapy, I administered a complete battery of psychological tests, including intelligence, achievement, and personality evaluation instruments. Additionally, as is good practice for any therapist, I confirmed through Alex's pediatrician that his health was sound and there were no apparent hormonal imbalances.

Alex's psychological evaluation indicated above-average intelligence, adequate reading and math skills, adequate ties with reality, but significant confusions about sexuality, complete with homosexual fantasies accompanied by feelings of guilt and anxiety about these. Furthermore, the testing indicated that Alex tended to be highly dependent on his mother, a dependency that he now resented but was reluctant to give up. In discussion with the mother I learned that she did, in fact, tend to be highly involved in all aspects of her son's life, describing herself as a "totally overprotective mother." She was perceptive enough to say that she knew she had to "let go" of her "baby," but that now she was so confused that she didn't know whether he needed more of her nagging or less.

Alex's father, a physician, tended to be less involved with the boy but was just as inconsistent as the mother in matters of discipline. He was thoroughly perplexed about what to do with Alex, having tried tutors, private school, long discussions, and threats to send the boy off to military school, none of which helped.

Alex did, however, like the private school he attended. It was only because the director of that school recommended me that Alex came to me for testing and then therapy. Initially, he tried to structure the situation by informing me that the whole problem was his mother's and that she should be the one coming. I replied that I partially agreed with that statement, but that I would have to do my job in my own way without Alex or anyone else telling me how to do it. I explained that I did work with parents, but that ordinarily I worked with the student individually as well. And after assurances that the sessions were entirely confidential, Alex and I embarked on a brief but intense therapeutic relationship.

Alex's psychological evaluation had indicated no imminent break with reality and no deep underlying depression. So I felt that within limits I could move quickly and zero in on what appeared to be a major problem, his own questions about himself as a male and the corollary problem of his attachment to, and need to detach from, his mother. He responded well, even seeming to welcome my interpretations regarding his psychological status, saying, "Well, thank God, someone's getting the picture at last!" This meant, for the most part, that Alex was getting the picture himself.

The young man's anxiety was much alleviated by several full and frank discussions about sex and sexuality, about natural and normal anxieties including various fantasies, both heterosexual and homosexual. We talked about the frequency of mutual masturbation among young males, about same-sex touching and how this was very common among girls but often considered taboo for boys (males being permitted bottom slaps and hugs, but usually only after great athletic exertions such as scoring a touchdown). We talked about how one's general sexuality often emerged first, with the young person often not having anyone of the opposite sex to play or practice with, thus making same-sex play or fantasy very likely. It appeared Alex had come to feel, even in our supposedly enlightened age, that sex was something one

did not talk about, want to watch, or want to participate in, unless married, and even then only for procreation. I disabused Alex of these ideas, saying that I did not even believe his parents thought in this manner. As it turned out, his parents actually had an open attitude about sex, though they felt inhibited about discussing sex with their children.

As usually happens, additional information about sexual identity difficulties and discussion of Alex's fears of "being a fag" helped lower some of his anxiety. This heightened his ability to concentrate on academic work. As Alex began to function again his parents became less anxious, and a home program was then developed.

Alex was becoming increasingly involved in using marijuana, about which his parents were disturbed. With Alex's permission, I met with the parents to discuss their values in this area. I told them my own feelings about the deleterious effects for this age group of the use of any drug in moderate to high dosage and frequency levels. The parents agreed with me, but they had been getting little support from liberal friends on this issue, and of course no support at all from Alex.

Again with Alex's permission, and after explaining to him the home program I was going to suggest, I met with his parents. Alex was invited to this meeting, to participate as much or as little as he saw fit. He decided not to attend, saying that he already understood the program (although he did not like it). He said he trusted me not to reveal anything about his homosexual fears. Of course I had no intention of discussing his sexual fears and fantasies, for I saw no good reason to do so. However, I did very much want the parents to be more consistent in their dealings with Alex, particularly about his use of marijuana in the home, his manner of going out whenever and for as long as he liked on school nights, and his handling of his anger toward them.

In conference with the parents, a home program was agreed upon which banned dope and paraphernalia such as "bongs" (water pipes through which marijuana can be

smoked) from the home. Alex's allowance was to be contingent upon adequate academic functioning at school and appropriate simple courtesy at home. We carefully attempted to stay within the "say what you mean and mean what you say" framework. That is, we avoided setting up contingencies of either reward or punishment that might prove unworkable for this family. For example, we stayed carefully away from any ultimatum, such as that Alex must behave in such and such a manner or he would have to go to boarding school. The parents were not ready to proceed on such a move, and at this time at any rate, I felt that it would simply serve to enrage Alex as well as heighten his general anxiety level.

To repeat, these guidelines were suggested *with Alex's prior knowledge and with his permission* (given very grudgingly).I felt that his permission was a manifestation of his basic need for reasonable structure, which the home program would provide.

Again with Alex's permission, I discussed his academic situation with the director of his school. This director said that Alex's work had sunk to a very low point and that ordinarily the school would have taken steps to dismiss such a poorly functioning student. The director had been unwilling to take such a step with Alex, sensing the boy's tenuous emotional stability and fearing to make things worse by expelling him. Alex and the school director and I carefully worked out a program wherein Alex was to receive supportive tutoring with an emphasis on study skills and organization of his academic work, which was to be reviewed weekly by the school staff. Alex understood that *improvement* would be the contingency by which the school would decide if he could remain as a student. If he continued as before, he would be warned within a week after his unsatisfactory review, and asked to leave the school if his work had not improved by the end of the following week. He agreed to these terms, though actually he was given no choice.

During the next month, Alex and his parents functioned well within this structure. Fine-tuning adjustments were

needed in some areas, such as how late he could stay out weekends, or if the parents should oversee his homework or leave this between Alex and the school. In the last matter I voted that homework should be left to Alex and the school. Everyone was pleased with the fact that at least now there was a plan with clear guidelines and structure within which to function.

In the work with Alex, we see a good illustration of the problem of values in psychotherapy. Most therapists are taught that the therapeutic process is to be kept as value-free as possible. The client or patient must be helped to see choices, possible resolutions of problems, and solutions to conflicts, but the therapist must not make the choices. I agree with this. But it is foolish to suppose that the values of the therapist do not intrude. From the location and style of his office to the manner of his talk and dress, not to mention the content of what he says and the type of questions he does or does not ask, the therapist's values blare out like billboards.

My solution to the question of values is to explain mine to the parents and the young person, then allow them to make their own value decisions about me. For example, I do not put a particularly high priority on academic success and college degrees for all students. It seems only fair for me to state things of this sort to the parents prior to their making counseling appointments for me with their child. A therapist should never undermine the parent-child relationship or confuse the young person by subtly advancing values or points of view that are opposite to those of the parents. For example, if parents prefer a highly structured, rather traditional prep school for their child, and the youngster can and does perform well in such an institution, the counselor risks great harm by advancing his own prejudices against such institutions. Or, if parents use alcohol and the counselor is into health and purity, the counselor may advance health-type thinking with the young person but must not attack or undermine the parents' behavior. If parents are abusing alcohol or other drugs, the therapist can help the young person

repudiate the use of drugs while tolerating the needs of others who use these substances as a solution to the stress of life.

All things are grist for the psychologist's mill if he regards himself as a teacher, as one who guides and instructs. Psychotherapy is not a medical science—one does not *heal*. Psychotherapy is an educational process. The therapist suggests possible courses of action, points out nuances of meaning, and challenges distorted thinking. He must also be understanding enough and humble enough to tolerate the rejection of his suggestions and interpretations.

Psychotherapy is an interesting profession, a kind of art, really. But discussions of the values of the therapist have already filled many books. It is enough here to say that the values of the therapist are important, since they do affect therapy. Along with reasonably adequate technical skills, the manner in which the therapist lives and what the therapist believes are influential forces in the therapeutic process.

MARCIA (17)

Marcia represents a good example of the way that basic feelings of insecurity and inferiority are heightened as the end of high school nears and going out into the world on one's own becomes more and more imminent. I had administered a complete battery of psychological tests to Marcia in her first year in high school and had discussed the results with Marcia and her parents. I pointed out that her average-level academic capacities and her strong perfectionist tendencies might mean trouble for her in the competitive high school she wished to attend. Her overall needs might be better met in a smaller, less academically pressuring environment. However, Marcia was a gregarious person and wanted a school large enough to have cheerleaders and a strong social scene. So for several years Marcia was, in fact, one of the cheerleaders for the school, also maintaining a good social life. Academically, she worked hard but achieved average results, sometimes dropping below average in particularly difficult subjects.

During her senior year Marcia began to increasingly feel the strain of choosing a college. Most of her friends were selecting schools such as UCLA, Stanford, or various eastern universities, while Marcia was consigned to the (for her) rather bleak prospect of attending one of the local community colleges. This, plus the prospect of losing her cheerleader's fiefdom, moving away from the protective wing of parents, and growing up in general, created severe anxieties in Marcia. She began to sleep poorly, worry constantly, lose weight, and manifest feelings of deep sadness. At this time, Marcia asked for counseling appointments.

In her initial visits with me Marcia was able to discuss her feelings of academic inferiority and how these feelings had been with her all her life. She stayed close to the surface of her feelings, allowing herself to make the "right" statements but not allowing much emotion to come through. When I pointed this out to her in our third or fourth visit, she replied with good insight, "Yeah, I have to blunt it by pretending not to care too much. But I know I do care. And I know I'm scared."

In later sessions, Marcia moved toward a fuller exploration of her needs and feelings, especially the painful separation process.

> I want to be a child forever. I rely on my mother. I don't feel that I can do anything right. Yet I also want to grow up and live away. I want to go to San Diego State. Yet I'm afraid of leaving. I don't like myself. I set my standards too high and get so moody. What's the matter with me? I know my mother didn't do all this [to me]. Why am I so afraid? Why am I so dependent and feel that I can't do without my parents?

We gradually moved into a discussion of the behaviorist's position that one can change one's feelings by changing one's behavior (as opposed to the more traditional psychodynamic viewpoint that feelings must change before behavior can be changed) and how this point of view might be useful for

Marcia. She decided that at least she would attempt to look and act more "up." She felt reassured when I told her how many high school seniors had sat in my office and offices all over the country literally crying the blues about leaving home. It was a hard time and her anxiety was understandable, but it should not be allowed to overwhelm her.

Over the next few sessions we discussed separation anxiety, general fears of the future, and how behaving in the manner in which her basic identity now seemed so inextricably intertwined could be considered a *negative personality*. Marcia defined herself as a moody, self-defeating, and sullen personality, despite the surface pep of the cheerleader facade. For Marcia, change could be seen more clearly now to mean changing deep aspects of her basic identity, clearly a frightening and challenging prospect.

Nonetheless, Marcia was game to keep trying. She attempted to put a better face on things, to react internally in an up rather than a down way to situations in her life. She kept a careful journal of her feelings and behaviors in order to critique herself better. She gradually came to see how past conditioning had evolved into her present fearful, depressed, and dependent pattern. More importantly, Marcia began to perceive ways of forging a new and more positive identity.

My process notes from a session at this time suggest the redundancy of the therapeutic process, inasmuch as virtually everything discussed in that session had been covered in previous conversations. Nonetheless, the "bridge analogy" that came out of the session was new, and this seemed to have a deep impact on her.

Process Notes   Marcia   December 1

M. spoke of being angry and depressed today, though not knowing why. We talked about the theory of depression (anger kept inside) but M. did not seem too interested. She stated that she was having difficulties with mother. Her boy friend was sarcastic. M. admitted

that she was, too. Crux of session came toward the end as I began to explain more fully (and M. began to really hear me for the first time) that it was my job to keep questioning and probing, helping individuals look at who they were, how they got that way, where they were going in life, and so on. I told M. that I felt part of her problems were her feelings of intellectual inferiority and that some of her anger was the fact that she felt not as bright as others in general, though she was pretty, athletic, and popular (gifts that many others might well envy). Also, that she was afraid of growing up, afraid of not being competent. M. totally agrees with these points and my analogy that it (growing up) is like crossing a bridge over a deep chasm. She is in the middle of the bridge between childhood and adulthood, and can't go back, afraid to go forward, and the winds are blowing, and the bridge is swaying. It's scary. My job is to go out and take people by the hand and lead them across. M. says that is a "great picture" and "really makes sense" to her. I tell her not to be afraid—to start writing her poems, keep her journal, and keep thinking through her fears, angers.

Marcia separated from parents and went away to college. She keeps in touch with me by letter. She is doing well academically and has a "a great social life." Marcia has, with help, made a successful life transition from dependent and frightened adolescent to adequately functioning young adult.

NICK (15)

Nick, a nice-looking, athletic boy, began therapy with me as a sophomore in high school. He was heavily involved in drugs, especially marijuana, and was creating extreme friction in the home with his quarrelsome nature, general defiance to parents, and often bullying tactics with younger sibs.

Relationships are often formed on slender threads. Nick, though initially resistant to any and all counseling, came to find me tolerable because I sailed a boat and enjoyed off-road motorcycles, or dirt bikes, as he did.

Initially, Nick and I spent many hours talking boats, bikes,

and cars. This was a necessary phase in our relationship, enabling me to establish good rapport. Of course while I was laying this foundation for a good relationship, I was also "wasting" a lot of expensive time. I was not able to turn the tide of conversation upstream into more significant psychological material at that point.

Eventually, my discomfort with this apparent standoff between us reached such proportions that I asked Nick's permission for a parent conference. He allowed the conference but said he would not attend. In the meeting, it quickly developed that Nick's parents were not at all displeased with the therapeutic situation. They said they had already noticed changes in Nick's attitude at home and at school. They urged me to continue doing whatever I was doing. They were very pleased to have me keep talking to Nick about boats or whatever. Such is the magic of therapy!

Actually, Nick's reaction is not uncommon among children and adolescents as they start a psychotherapeutic relationship. The reasons probably differ from person to person as to why changes in attitude and behavior begin to take place even though nothing in counseling seems to have triggered it. I believe that some of the significant factors in the young person's therapeutic gain involve (1) general rapport with a caring adult, (2) relief that someone is in his or her corner, and (3) the gain from intergenerational contact when the older person considers the younger person as an equal, though less experienced in many areas of life. It is very important for the therapist to treat the adolescent just as he would an adult client (for example, offering a cup of coffee, a handshake, and so on).

Working with children, adolescents, and adults, I have found that teenagers tend to be extremely sensitive to subtle status cues. If I have been working with a child and we have been building a model or playing with Legos, these materials can be left in view on a table if my next client is another child or an adult, but not if an adolescent is scheduled next. The adolescents' ambivalence about childhood-adulthood seems

to make them highly reactive to whether or not they are still considered children (by me or by others). Consequently, for the adolescent my office must be warm and friendly, but definitely "adult."

Nick and I finally did shade our discussions into more meaningful psychological material. Nick began to dredge up highly painful memories of his early school years. Although he had attended a progressive elementary school, the school had not been helpful in assisting him with his visual-perceptual difficulties and his resulting academic problems. The school had even resisted the intervention of outside remedial educational therapy, taking the position that Nick would gradually outgrow the perceptual problems and they could then teach him the basic skills.

Nick's parents, however, were wise enough to get specialized reading tutoring assistance for him despite the school's negative attitude toward it. Nonetheless, learning to read was a struggle for Nick and because of it he suffered from the guilt and frustration that accompanied his numerous academic failures.

As Nick and I reconstructed the situation in our therapy sessions, it became apparent that he had essentially built a wall around his feelings. He could recall, at age eight or nine, being humiliated by a teacher and laughed at by classmates over one of his reading mistakes, and deciding "no one will ever hurt my feelings again." This evolved over the years to "no one will ever know me at all." Nick was so perceptive that at once upon telling me this, he noted that he had just let his guard down and let me know him a bit. This led to a discussion of whether or not I or anyone could ever be trusted with his feelings.

Over a period of time, Nick came to see that in order to have anything more than very shallow relationships, he had to trust others to some extent. Almost simultaneously with this series of discussions, Nick abandoned his previously aloof attitude toward girls (girls liked Nick and he had had sexual encounters, but had allowed himself no emotional

attachment) and became much more seriously involved with one of the girls at his school.

Nick and I then moved in our discussions into a period in which he was able to recall and then ventilate much anger over his past treatment in school and his present feelings of fear of the future. His deep feelings of academic inferiority caused him to shy away from really committing himself to getting good grades in high school. He could not bear to consider college, or even employment in his father's business, feeling that he simply was not competent. For a long while Nick held to a decision to become a ski bum and a beach bum—depending on the season—while dealing pot and other drugs.

I accepted Nick's plans for his future without much comment, noting only that I too had been a beach bum for six months after graduating from college and until receiving my draft notice had had no plans to do anything except surf, play volleyball, and drive a beer truck once a week for spending money.

Nick gradually came around to asking me why I had become a beach bum and had not wanted to make something of myself immediately. I answered honestly that I had not been much concerned with making something of myself since I already thought I was "something" (in the positive sense), and in any case felt no compelling pressure to rush into a career since I was already living like a millionaire on the beaches of Southern California.

During this series of discussions Nick began exploring possible jobs he felt he might be able to do, and even began to talk about going to college after high school. He took a job teaching surfing for a boy's club and was very well thought of in this position. At about the same time he began to excel in athletics at his school, becoming something of a leader. We discussed his leadership abilities with their potential for misuse.

"I never really thought I'd be chosen captain of my football team. That's more responsibility. The other kids
look up to me a lot now. I know that. That's why I get
griped when the coach doesn't know what he's doing or
seem to give much of a damn. It gets to me when the
guys don't try."

(You try, they'll follow your lead. If it's important to
you to play well, it will become so for the coach. Teams
and armies often have imcompentent leaders. Just think
about it, let it be a lesson. Listen, *there is no competition
out there!* Half the world is a bunch of incompetent
boobs. Anyone who has some skill and some intelligence and will *try,* will care about what they are doing,
will be a standout.)

"Yeah. You've said that so much I've come to believe it.
Sometimes I even hear our conversations when I'm just
sitting alone and thinking. But what about this leadership thing? The younger guys, especially, will follow
me. They think it's cool to smoke a doobie before class,
after school, before a game. That's not cool, that's
stupid."

(You did the same thing.)

"I was stupid, I'll admit. I guess I'll just have to kick
some ass to get some sense into their heads."

(Maybe just setting a different example will have the
same or better result than kicking ass.)

"Whatever. Anyway, I can see that I've got to clean up
my act. I'm not dealing [selling marijuana or other
drugs] anymore. I don't intend to do [take] any of the
hard stuff again. Funny how you work yourself out of
it. I used to do it all, now just pot. I wouldn't even use
that before a game. I can't believe those dumb jocks
smoking Js [joints] before practice. If I lean on them,
and if I have 'put down' [stopped smoking pot] and they
know it, maybe they'll stop, too."

Nick graduated from high school, a class leader in all respects. He decided to go on to college and chose a small school in the mountains where he could study and ski. At this point, Nick has largely overcome the defeatism and anger created by his severe learning problems in the early school years.

With Marcia and Nick I emphasized parent conferencing far less than with Alex. However, there were parent conferences on an intermittent basis, especially with Nick during his first year in high school. With middle- or older-adolescents I tend to do less parent conferencing unless the problem largely involves difficulties between members of the family. In that case I might offer family conferences, conferences with one or both parents and the adolescent, or maybe between my adolescent client and the member of the family with whom he or she seems to be having the most difficulties, such as a sibling, a stepparent, or a parent in a divorce situation.

As a general rule, in my work with adolescents I focus on the development of a person's innate potential as a person, with strong consideration being given to whatever environment the individual is in. That is, what type of home situation the teenager is in plays a part. Is there a divorce? If so, what is the nature of the relationship between the parents? Have the parents remarried? The therapist needs also to be aware of the different neighborhood pressures and different types of pressures from school to school throughout the city. Is the school a high academic pressure school? Is it a high drug-infested school? In short, the therapist is trying to figure out how the individual teenager with whom he is working fits in, or does not fit in, with school and home environments and what impact these environments may be having on the young person.

Since there appears to be a natural tendency in most of us to blame others for our own difficulties, it is common for the adolescent client to heap the blame for most or even all difficulties on parents, teachers, or others. When this is the case,

I usually attempt gradually (very gradually) to confront the young person with the fact that he or she is blaming others and that the tendency to do this seems frequent. I then pose the question, "At what point does one become responsible for one's own behavior?" And I confront the patient (often repeatedly) with: "No matter who did what to you up to this point, it does no good to blame others. Your life is in your hands now. The decisions are yours and the consequences, good or bad, are yours to be proud of or to suffer with."

This is in line with my belief that more and more the responsibility for the actions of adolescents must be shifted over to them. Being a parent myself, I realize how difficult it can be to allow your teenagers to be hurt by their own irresponsibility (for example, getting fired for not going to work on time; receiving poor grades for not turning in homework; not getting into the college of choice because applications were not made out properly and sent in on time; losing driving privileges because of too many tickets or too many accidents; having a bicycle stolen because someone was too lazy to put it in the garage; and so on and so on). Still, it is generally best to allow the adolescent to take the consequences, as difficult as that may be—for the parent as much as for the child.

There are, of course, exceptions to this point of view. For one thing, as a parent you must reflect and find your own tolerance limits. Some parents actually cannot tolerate poor grades or having their child flunk out of school. These parents, as previously noted, may provide various rewards for grades. Grades obtained under such conditions seem to me to be of dubious value, but parents who provide such contingencies obviously have strong needs that only their children can fulfill. These needs may be extensions of the parents' needs, rather than a genuine parental feeling for the good of the child. With other parents, it may be poorly thought out parenting behavior, rather than deep psychological needs. The motives are pure but the techniques seem questionable.

No parent should, however, allow any apparently self-destructive behavior to continue without attempting to make some move to prevent it. Currently, drug involvement appears to be the most potentially self-destructive behavior among young people. Consequently, parents with knowledge of moderate to heavy drug use by their young would do well to step in and try to provide appropriate professional assistance, such as outpatient psychotherapy or, in extreme cases, a detoxification (detox) program or inpatient care at a psychiatric hospital.

Parents are often confused about the precise point at which they should intervene and, if they do get into the act, what steps to take. There are no hard and fast answers. Each case must be taken on its own merit, considering the degree of seriousness and the parental tolerance limits. Some parents begin talking hospitalization or boarding school upon first discovering that the child has become involved in pot, Quaaludes, Valium, alcohol, heroin, or whatever. Others are more tolerant or perhaps less anxious, and they move toward less drastic resolutions, at least initially. John's mother, it may be recalled from an earlier chapter, simply could not tolerate his use of pot in or out of the home. Her intense reactions to her son's use of drugs created such a volatile situation within the household that separation became necessary.

Each therapist working with adolescents must find his own tolerance level. I start each therapeutic relationship with a discussion of the confidentiality of our sessions. I state that the teenager can tell anyone anything about what we discuss, but I can tell no one anything. There are a couple of major exceptions. I must now, by California law, inform any person my client is threatening with bodily injury, and I must attempt to stop my client if suicide appears imminent. And though there is no law on this matter, I tell each of my adolescent patients that if he or she starts making use of any of the hard drugs on anything like a regular basis, I will at my own discretion and for his or her safety inform parents or anyone else who may be in a position to help stop such

behavior. Thus, once the adolescent client tells me about drug involvement, I have to make the decision about what to do next. Is this information a cry for help? Does the patient want hospitalization? Or is this a plea for us to work on the problem and contain it and resolve it? If so, can we do it? And if we try and fail, at what point do I decide the outpatient program should be escalated or confidentiality broken? And so on. In these cases, the therapist's course is anything but clear, and one treads very fine lines indeed.

And what about a client's actions that might seriously damage another person emotionally? Or which, as with drugs, are illegal? What is the proper therapeutic maneuver with an older teenager who reveals that he is engaged in seducing 11-to-12-year-old boys? If one breaks confidentiality and goes to the parents or the police, what will come of that? The adolescent may be made to remain in therapy or attend special treatment schools, but when he reaches legal age in another half year or so, who will then make him come to therapy or any other program? Is the risk of revelation greater than the risk of making the person distrustful of the only currently known useful helping technique—psychological counseling?

Given the fact that there is usually little that parents can do either to help or to hinder this more serious sort of behavior, a good case can be made for never informing parents or anyone else except in the situations covered by law—*imminent* homicide or suicide. Not all therapists are in agreement with the law, pointing out that its likely effect is that clients will hide information that might otherwise have been discussed and resolved within the therapeutic framework. There are, of course, no easy answers in these situations. The nature of the adolescent, not a child but not yet an adult, compounds and complicates already difficult decisions. Yet every therapist who works with this age group must make such decisions.

As a general rule, adolescents are among the most difficult patients or clients, whichever term one prefers, for the psychotherapist. Younger children are usually easy to

establish rapport with. And adults come to therapy because of some aspect of their life that troubles them, and they are searching for understanding and relief.

Adolescents, however, are often truculent and surly, obstinately wanting no contact with the adult world, especially with a "shrink." Nevertheless, the general rule of thumb in my profession is not to accept adolescents as patients unless they express some willingness to work on their problems. This seems folly to me and I believe no such demands should be made. Few adolescents will even admit that they have any problems that cannot be blamed on parents, school, and the attitudes of the adult world. Also, adolescents tend to shy away from commitments that smack of long-term, possibly in-depth emotional exploration.

I regard myself as a *tutor*, a psychological tutor who can be useful to the adolescent merely through repeated exposure (weekly sessions) over a period of time (usually several months or more) in a neutral and benign setting (my office). So it is not necessary that my young patients "admit" to having problems. All I ask is that we engage in civil discourse. If they will permit me that, I will teach them much about themselves and about people in general. In fact, I sincerely believe that a tolerant adult who knows something of underlying psychological principles could be useful to an adolescent even if the young person participated only minimally in the therapeutic exchange.

So-called intensive psychotherapy aimed at exploring the "deepest level of feelings," *may* have some validity in some instances with adults. In my judgment, it has almost no validity whatsoever with adolescents who are attempting to find their identities and settle themselves down psychologically. They hardly need a therapist poking and probing into the hot coals of their psyches to fan further the already quickening flames. Rather than intensive therapy, I prefer long-term contact between the young person and a mature adult counselor. The counselor should have the simple and straightforward posture that what he or she has to teach

about human behavior is a good thing for anyone to know more about. The counselor's attitude should also be that of an "honest broker" between the teenager and others—an advocate, though not one who offers uncritical acceptance of all of the young person's behavior.

Like the parent who used the "never say no but give me a chance to discuss it" method, a counselor working with adolescents cannot say no. The therapist has no actual power over the young person, but can only help examine behavior in terms of its underlying meanings and its consequences. The therapist must also assist the youngster toward a better understanding of the motives of other people, such as parents and teachers, and thus by extension toward a better understanding of human behavior.

In addition to all of this, I try to bring the following four major dimensions into the relationship with my adolescent clients, as I believe all therapists should try to do.

Acceptance as an equal, though not a peer. I see the adolescent's difficulties as serious, but not impossible to resolve. I accord adolescents the same dignity and status as I accord adults. I accept whatever they say without valuation or criticism, though all issues are open for appraisal and discussion.

I offer *practical assistance,* as from a more experienced person to a less experienced one. The young person may know how to go through channels at school on some matters, but it may be that the manner in which he or she intends to resolve a particular moral or legal problem is partially steeped in ignorance of the facts, the issues, or the laws. I offer assistance in the form of discussions of pros and cons or basic information, *not* in doing for the young person directly.

Setting realistic goals is something with which most of us need assistance at one point or another in our lives, and adolescents usually need such assistance even more. Some young people will attempt too much, which sets the stage for failure. Other teenagers will not dare to try enough. They need to learn more about what they can do and experience

the exhilaration that can come from effectively using their talents.

Encouragement to dream goes hand in hand with setting goals. Without a dream, reality often fails to materialize. Sometimes adults fail to realize that a young person's dreams, no matter how wild, grandiose, or farfetched, are that person's way of trying on ideas, of vicariously going down this path or up that road, but *all in the mind.* If adolescents allow you into their dreams, then you are indeed in a rare position to be useful to them. For you can then, in a gentle way, offer feedback from your own experience with how things work in this world, how one certainly must have a goal but must start somewhere and develop and follow some plan.

No one of the above points is the exclusive domain of the psychotherapist. As I have repeated throughout the book, adults have to help young people grow up. Such help comes in many different ways and, if the youngster is lucky, from many different people. The more the young know about this world, especially about human behavior, the less they fear. The less they fear, the more competently and confidently they can forge ahead into the next phase of life.

ABOUT THE AUTHOR

James E. Gardner, Ph.D., is noted for his diagnostic and psychotherapeutic work with children and adolescents and for his counseling of parents. His impressive background includes such positions of responsibility as: Director of the Children's Center in Venice, California, Chief Psychologist at Children's Hospital of Los Angeles, Director of the Psychological Center of Los Angeles, consultant to various hospitals and schools, and Chairperson of the Ethics Committee of the California State Psychological Association. Dr. Gardner has taught at USC and UCLA and has published many articles in scientific journals. He wrote and developed a film on rearing children for *Psychology Today* and is the author of an important training book in his field: *Paraprofessional Work with Troubled Children.* He has raised five teenagers of his own.